American Kabuki

A novel by

Sheridan Tatsuno

DREAMSCAPE GLOBAL
San Francisco, California

Also on Amazon by

SHERIDAN TATSUNO

Non-Fiction
The Technopolis Strategy
Created in Japan
In the Valley of Digital Dreams
The Gaiapolis Strategy

Poetry
San Francisco Cantos (poetry)
Land of a Thousand Dreams (poetry)
Chaos (poetry)
Ghost Cities, Floating Cities (poetry)

Novels

Virtually SF Series
Virtually San Francisco (Tenderloin)
Uniquely San Francisco (SOMA)
Soulfully San Francisco (Fillmore)
Divinely San Francisco (East Bay)
Zenfully San Francisco (Japantown)
Virally San Francisco (UCSF Mission Bay)
Fashionably San Francisco (Chinatown)
Beatfully San Francisco (North Beach)
Haightfully San Francisco (Haight Ashbury)
Cosmically San Francisco (Virtual Mars)

Gaiapolis

Japantown Series
Kimono Minds
American Kabuki

The characters and names in this novel are purely fictitious
composites of attendees at San Francisco events.
Any resemblance to real people is purely coincidental.

ISBN: 9798858458173

A dying downtown
American Kabuki
A gift from Japan!

Part 1

The Inferno

1

GHOST CITY

Yerba Buena ghosts
Rise from our Barbary Coast
Haunting the homeless

San Francisco is dying, a ghost city like Colma, with its miles of cemeteries. Few commuters come downtown, which is filled with birds scrapping for crumbs in dark canyons. I venture forth from Japantown to meet Maker friends at the few remaining tech events. Covid-19 is over, but downtown is scary. The streets are filled with the homeless, trash, needles, feces and gangs. I wear running shoes and never bring my laptop. The police are scarce so theft rings operate freely. The only safe spaces are the Ferry Building and Moscone Center. The rest of downtown is a depressing netherworld of wary pedestrians and lost tourists. Our dystopian nightmare is so grim that even Hollywood crews shooting SF Noir thrillers are afraid of assaults and thefts, so they arm themselves with phalanxes of bodyguards. Despite the costs and inconvenience, it's more realistic shooting here than creating dystopian worlds on LA sets. The City is begging for businesses so cannabis shops are thriving like weeds. Our mayor, Tiffany Wong-Gonzalez, a Mission bro and former Navy pilot, is an eternal optimist, bragging about our film renaissance. "We are Digital Hollywood!" is plastered all over town but few people see the graffiti-covered posters. We are the laughingstock of the media, pariahs living in our ultra-blue bubble telling ourselves how great we are.

Why am I, Brad Morioka, a crazy robotics nut, still going

downtown? Am I a masochist, a voyeur, a hardcore techie hoping for an economic miracle or am I just insane? I plead guilty to all of the above. Nobody in his right mind goes downtown anymore. Tech giants have hightailed to Texas, Arizona and Nevada. Office workers are nowhere to be seen. The Old San Francisco of booming tech companies, lavish parties, and flowing bars from the Roaring 2010s is over. Like the market crashes of 1973, 1980, 1990, 2000 and 2008, everything has stopped. Our digital wonderland has vanished like the mid-day fog. We stand a Naked City with miles of empty office towers. The only sounds are clanging cable cars climbing halfway to the stars on Powell Street. We were once a glittering city on the hill, but now the City is a ghost town with lights out, like photos from World War II.

"Brad," says Mari. "Wake up! Are you OK?"

I turn to my sister Mariko, who is dressed in her typical Goth outfit of black leathers and motorcycle boots, with her hair raked back like the screaming banshee on her jacket patch.

"You look like a zombie."

"I'm just bummed out. I went downtown. It's a total shit hole. Needles and crap all over. The City never cleans it up."

"What else is new? We've got progressives and reactionaries jamming Mayor Tiff from all sides."

"She's trying."

"What? With the National Guard and recycled policies that don't work? Visitors, gangs and city folks aren't stupid. They can see through her cant. Can't do this. Can't do that. You can't do anything downtown anymore with all the regulations and approvals. I'm thinking of moving to Oakland. At least they'll approve my shop in weeks, not months like here."

"They've got problems too."

"At least they welcome artists, not just techies who aren't coming back anyway. This town needs a total reset."

"Any ideas?"

"I thought you Maker guys and our gamer mayor had all the creative ideas and money for tech. We artists starve."

I gaze at the City's fantasyland photos of downtown, as if it was the most wonderful place in the world, but everyone knows the truth. It's all a façade like Hollywood. Nobody but Tiff's PR handlers believes her hype. It will take a miracle to revive our

Sleeping Beauty.

"What are you going to do?" asks Mari. "Open your Maker shop somewhere else?"

"Maybe. Mom's shop is too crowded and she's all about kimonos, not robots and cool Maker stuff, so I'm looking around town."

I admire my growing collection of robots of all shapes and sizes, arrayed like mom's Japanese kimonos. We're both inveterate collectors, two birds of different feathers. My family is a bunch of crazy collectors. Mari is into Goth motorcycle helmets, leather jackets and pants, and boots. Emi collects anime cosplay outfits that overflow her closet. Yumi is creating an awesome collection of "uncanny valley" virtual reality (VR) and artificial reality (AR) avatars for her Cal consciousness tech projects. Our house is packed with our growing collections so we have to move if we want to start our own businesses.

Mom is the ultimate collector. Her exploding collection of kimonos is overwhelming us. She has so many kimonos that we are drowning in them. We like her zeal but we don't have space or time for our own passions. It's decision time for my sisters and me -- move out or shut up. Mom wants me to stay since I handle her logistics, lighting and pop-ups, but it's wearing me out. I need my own space.

"Well, Maker Man," says Mari. "Where are you headed?"

"I don't know. Japantown Center has foot traffic but it's costly and I hear tenants are getting kicked out if they miss a few rent payments."

"That's biz. Pay up or out you go."

Mari and I look at each with frustration. We dream about launching our creative ventures, but it looks dim given the recession and the City's collapse. We might as well be in Detroit; at least they're growing gardens to survive. Here, we can't do anything new or creative. It is the City's way or the highway. Most of my friends are taking the highway.

2

KABUKI BANK

San Francisco high
My Osaka dreams still live
Despite the slowdown

My father is a brave Osaka banker. He has big dreams of expanding
our bank in America. When I was little, he talked about moving to
San Francisco, our sister city. We would grow by being different
from other Japanese banks; we would serve Korean, Chinese and
other Asian companies since my father loves gamers and electronics.
He is still a kid. He grew up near Akihabara in Tokyo and spent his
weekends playing with new games and gadgets. His friends came
from all over Asia. Our apartment looks like a toy store. Robots,
game boxes, manga and mobile gizmos fill every shelf and counter. I
enjoy playing with them, but my dream is fashion design and writing
haiku. I want to study green fashion, which Mayor Tiffany Wong-
Gonzalez is promoting to build the City's tiny fashion industry. I
want to be part of her Green Fashion Renaissance! I am enrolled in a
fashion school downtown, which only has a few students left since
Covid-19, but foreign students are returning, especially from Asia, so
we don't feel alone anymore. We wish more people would come
downtown, but it's not happening. Dad is losing bank customers and
office renters. Unless the City turns around soon, he may have to sell
his office tower and we will have to return to Osaka. That would be
terrible! We both want to stay, but mom wants to go home. She's
tired of hearing dad complain and she is afraid of going out because
of all the filth, crime and attacks. She calls those people "yabanjin"
(barbarians). She prefers Osaka, which is clean and much safer. I try

to convince them to stay.

"Ayako, mom is right," my father says. "Aren't you afraid of staying?"

"I'm OK. I go out with my fashion friends. We avoid the Tenderloin and Civic Center Plaza. We only visit safe places -- Japantown, the Haight, the Mission, Union Square, North Beach, Clement Street and Cow Hollow."

"Why so many places?"

"To gather ideas and materials. Shops are looking for regenerative fashion concepts since the mayor is offering grants to new designers."

"Regenerative fashion? What's that?"

"We can only use recycled textiles and second-hand clothes."

"Used clothes? Why would anybody buy it?"

"City kids love recycled clothes. They can't afford new stuff and hate copycat fast fashion. It pollutes the world."

"But Tokyo is the fashion capital, not San Francisco."

"In fast fashion, even Tokyo kids are wearing eco fashions. It's a new trend."

"You know fashion better than me. I'm just an old guy who likes electronics."

I like my dad since he is open-minded like Bay Area folks, not like my mom who always want things done "chanto" like Japan. I tell her we aren't living in Japan, but she always complains about the poor product quality and service here. I tell her America is better for new ideas, but she likes the old ways. She is so traditional that we argue all the time, but it's no use. At least my dad loves the City even though it's weird and crazy. Mom thinks we are both weird and crazy.

3

PRICED OUT

My bros are psyched up
Makers conquering the world
With cool stuff on fire!

We Makers never take no for an answer. I talk to the Japan Trade Mall folks about renting a small pop-up area for my robots and my buddies, but we are quoted outrageous prices, plus a huge deposit bigger than our annual income. We try to negotiate it down, but no luck; cash upfront or no deal. We are pissed off and ask the Youth Task Force for help, but they shrug their shoulders. Their budget is allocated to existing shops and Japanese newcomers. It totally sucks, but that's Cash Francisco. You either have the cash or go elsewhere. That's why everyone is leaving town. We can't afford luxury-priced digs sagging with age. Where are we going to go? Half of our friends are looking at the East Bay and Sacramento, but they're getting pricey too. At this rate, we'll all end up in Texas. Ugh, too hot and boring for my tastes.

"What should I do?" I ask Mari. "It's Oakland or all points east."

"That's what I'm thinking. Even the Lower Haight is way over my head and it's dying too. Only a few ritzy shops run by trust fund babies."

"Definitely not us. And mom's shop is way too crowded. How about pop ups?"

"My biker buddies and I are trying but it's tough finding decent space on the right days and locations. They only show us dead areas."

"So it's mom's shop or nothing."

"Unfortunately, that's the reality. It sucks but what else are we going to do? I don't want to spend my thirties living with mom and her kimonos. I'll go nuts. Anything but kimonos. I'd rather go on the road with my buddies than hang around frilly kimonos."

That's the harsh reality of the City today: cash or out! What ever happened to the City's Summer of Love passion for artists and great rock music? Where did all the crazy love go? The only thing opening today is fancy cannabis shops all tricked out with high-cost smokes, pills, and pipes. None of my sisters and I are into grass, just mom and dad from their highs in the 1990s. We cannot afford it anyway. Fashion and robots are our drugs of choice.

So we need a solution and fast. Maybe mom has an idea: Kabuki Bank. She knows the owner who gave her a small loan last year. Perhaps he will finance our pop-ups. No risk in asking.

Mom arranges a meeting and we walk into the tiny bank office, ready to be rejected. To our surprise, the owner, Taro Yamaguma, welcomes us and invites us to sit down, offering green tea to ease our nervousness.

"So you need a small loan to run pop-ups this summer? How much?"

"Just five thousand dollars for both of us," says Mari. "So we can lease spaces, buy materials and pay assistants."

"Not much. Have you done pop-ups before?"

"Only in mom's shop, but we're expanding and she's crowded so we need to find our own space."

Yamaguma-san inspects us like a fashion designer, analyzing our hair, clothes and posture. We sit up ramrod straight. He smiles.

"I think it will work. I like both of you. I like your mother. She's from Kansai too so we get along well. You're all set. Come in tomorrow and I'll set up your accounts."

Mari and I exhale. We love his kindness and generosity. Nobody else trusts our business judgment. We love Kansai folks!

4

FAST AND FURIOUS CITY

I'm so late again
Hurry, hurry, hurry now
Most important date!

City people are always in a rush. Ever since Covid-19 lockdowns ended, traffic has gotten worse. I'm afraid to walk across the street. Drivers are crazy here, much worse than Osaka. They almost run you over. Always rushing here and there since they are late. Why don't they leave home earlier? Americans are always "fashionably late." It's a custom here, like taking forever to walk cross a busy street. So American! They live in their tiny bubbles unaware of others. Oh well, that's why I like Americans. They're open, free and innocent, like children, not shy and careful like us Japanese. That's why I came to SF. It's busy like Osaka but without all the rules. People here chase their dreams even as adults. They don't understand the word "no," but "just do it!" My father says San Francisco is "Disneyland for adults," where adults act like kids. I like the "Tinker Bell" women with pink, yellow and purple hair and the "Peter Pan" guys with beards in their thirties and forties who live in "man camps" like college students. They look like the original 49er gold miners in their blue jeans and work shirts pursuing their fortunes. The transgenders make us all look old and boring with their rainbow outfits and Korean makeup. Mayor Tiffany wears green gowns to formal events using hemp, recycled textiles and new biomaterials. They all inspire me because they encourage me to pursue my dreams and never give up. They are so free spirited, so American.

But all that freedom has its negatives. I was walking along

Market Street and chatting with my fashion classmate when it happened. A guy racing somewhere didn't stop in time and hit me. I was knocked down and my leg was pinned under the wheel. It hurt so much! I screamed until the ambulance came. Blood was everywhere on the street. My classmate fainted. People rushed to help. Medics lifted me and put me into the ambulance. Then I blacked out…

My mother and father sit next to my hospital bed. I open my eyes. My mother holds my hands and cries with joy. The light is so bright that I shut my eyes. My head hurts and my body even more. I try to smile but everything hurts. My left leg feels tingly but I feel nothing in my right leg. I put my hand down to touch my right leg. Nothing! I feel nothing, just the sheets. Where is my leg? Am I dreaming? I cry out, hoping it's just a nightmare.

Mother hugs me tightly. I feel her warm breath against my cheeks. She cries so hard that I begin crying too. We are both crying so my father hugs us. I open my eyes. His eyes are wet too. We are all crying together. We Japanese usually don't cry in public, only when it hurts a lot. I close my eyes, happy we are here together as a family then it all goes dark.

It has been two weeks since my accident. The guy who hit me was texting so he didn't see me. It's so common now. I wish they would ban phone use in cars. Everybody drives around half the time using maps and texting, always in their bubbles. I wish cars would automatically shut off if a phone was used, then drivers wouldn't cause so many accidents.

My father and mother sit next to my bed looking worried. Did the doctor tell them something serious? My father smiles but I can tell it is bad news.

"Ayako, your mother and I have decided. I'm closing our bank and returning to Osaka."

"What! You can't do that. I want to go back to school!"

"It's too dangerous for you to stay here. There are just too many crimes and speeding cars. It's not safe here anymore."

"But what about your dream for the bank?"

"It's over. San Francisco is dead. I'm losing customers. Many have left town. Others are going bankrupt."

"What about my fashion dreams? Don't I get a say?"

"Shikagata ga nai (our way of saying "It can't be helped — or forget it."). We can't change the City. We need to go back to Osaka where it's safer and you can get an artificial leg. I know prosthetic companies."

"I don't want a Kansai leg! I want a California leg!"

"It's too risky. We need to go home. Mom and I think it's best for all of us."

"Please, dad, let's stay! Anything so we can live our dreams."

"I wish we could, but it's — difficult now."

My father was always the confident guy who never gave up and always hung in — "gaman" Japanese style — and would bounce back like a Daruma, so I'm surprised he wants to quit. This is only a setback. I can get a new leg and continue studying. I have to convince mom. She makes all the decisions anyway.

"Mom, please let us stay! Please! We can do it. I know we can."

"Life is not always so easy, Ayako. Your dad and I think it's best for you, for all of us. San Francisco is fun, but Kansai is home. We should go home."

I beg both of them to stay, but they refuse. I need to think of something, anything, to convince them. I know dad wants to stay so I'll work on him. He came because we both wanted to live in SF. Mom wanted to stay with her friends in Osaka. It won't be easy but I'll figure out a way to get a new leg here and convince dad to stay. Maybe move to a smaller office or do something amazing, like he always wanted to do when we arrived.

5

PROSTHETICS

3D is The Way
Zen Buddhism in VR
We print overnight!

One thing great about being a Maker is that you can make anything you can imagine. My buddies and I got a cheap 3D printer and are playing around with it. We print toys, car parts, decals, tennis rackets and anything people want. Our little business is doing so well that we are getting orders from friends all over town. Steve Durbin, a veteran and gamer who advises Mayor Tiffany on the City's cultural district recovery, is the master. His Virtual Fillmore, which he built using VR, is so popular that he went public a few years ago; he is our business advisor. We've been talking about how to revive downtown since it's a total disaster. Only half of the commuters are returning to offices so bars, restaurants and shops have shut down. It's a total ghost town. Mayor Tiffany needs to grab victory from the jaws of defeat quickly or she will lose the next election. I tell Steve that Makers can help since our work requires physical presence and interaction. You can create 3D models online, but you need to print them somewhere so we might as well use the empty offices. We're perfect for saving downtown, but only if the City helps us.

"What do you guys need?" he asks.

"Everything. Seed funding, cheap or free space, and freedom to create anything we want."

"That might be a little hard with the huge budget deficit."

"Do you want to save downtown or not? All my friends are moving to Oakland and the East Bay since they're inviting Makers, not drowning them in red tape like SF."

"I'll ask Mayor Tiffany. By the way, can you print prosthetics?"

"Why? Do your vet buddies need them?"

"No, a Japanese girl named Ayako lost her leg when a car hit her last week. Her father runs Kabuki Bank, but he's thinking of selling his office tower and returning to Osaka. The City can't afford it. We need him to stay."

"Yamaguma-san! He just gave my mother a small loan for her fall fashion show. What does he want?"

"Ayako wants a tattoo leg, not a typical bulky one."

"I'm on it. When can I meet her?"

"Tomorrow evening after dinner?"

Talk about manna from heaven. I hate schadenfreude, but Ayako's request is the best thing that could have happened. A tattoo leg -- that's awesome. Better than printing toy race cars. We can show off our creative chops! I couldn't have thought of a better challenge. We will make Ayako proud.

Steve arranges for me to meet Yamaguma-san and Ayako after dinner. We go to his office on Market Street near the cable car turnaround. It's dark and scary, like a noir movie, with homeless people bundled under heavy blankets. Steve leads me upstairs. I jump. Scowling Kabuki masks leer at us in the lobby. Yamaguma-san definitely knows how to grab people's attention. My mom says he's the unofficial promoter of our flagging Osaka-San Francisco sister city program, which has hit bumps over the Korean comfort women controversy. But that's politics; we're worried about business and saving downtown.

Yamaguma-san welcomes us cordially, but you can see the stress on his face. He looks like a defeated man so I feel extra motivated to help Ayako and his bank.

"Thank you for coming quickly," he says, bowing deeply. "I appreciate your help."

"Anything I can do to repay your loan to my mom," I reply.

He guides us to a back office where Ayako is seated with her mother on a sofa. Her mother gets up and bows. Ayako tries to get up, but has trouble balancing on one leg. I feel really bad for all of them. They expect so much from me.

"I'm pleased to meet you," I say in formal Japanese.

I speak Kansai dialect, but am shy around folks from Osaka since my mother is from Kyoto, where our speaking is softer and more nuanced than Osaka's more lively, direct and business-like chatter.

"We are so happy you can help Ayako," says her mother, holding back her emotions. "We hear you print tattoo legs."

"I print tattoo mannequins for my sister Mariko, who runs a Goth fashion business and specializes in cool San Francisco tattoos."

"And prosthetics?"

"Just mannequins so far."

"Can you print this?" asks Ayako.

She pulls out her phone and clicks on Mari's webpage of 3D tattoos that I printed for a recent Goth party. Ayako points to a tattoo mannequin of a 1960s hippie girl frolicking and dancing in Golden Gate Park, an idea I got from Botticelli's "La Primavera," my favorite Renaissance painting.

"Can you print a see-through tattoo leg for me?"

"Yes, but why see-through?"

"It would be lighter and look like leggings, not a stump."

A hollow 3D leg? It never dawned on me that anybody might want one, but business is business.

"Whatever you want. What color?"

"A pinkish cream, like my legs."

"Got it."

I look at her normal leg and it's light and pinkish so I take a photo so I can match the color. For me, 3D printing a hollow leg is a no-brainer, but getting the shape and tattoo design right will be harder. I'll need my Osaka sculptor friend, Yoko Hamabe, to help with the leg shape. She sculpts all types of solar sculptures so she can sculpt anything. Mari can help with the tattoo.

"You've got a deal. I just need to measure your normal leg and I'll print your new leg by next week. Is that OK?"

"Freaking awesome!"

"Where did you learn those words?"

"From Steven. He said it when you said you could help me."

Steve grins like a Cheshire cat. This is huge for me since Yamaguma-san is the only banker willing to take a risk on us tiny ventures. Without Kabuki Bank, my mother's Kimono Minds shop would have gone bankrupt during the Covid-19 shutdown. So there is hope. I hope I can help Ayako look good. My Maker friends and I want to open 3D printing shops and his half-empty office tower is perfect – right next to the cable cars so we can hawk our stuff to tourists in his street-level window. If we can do that, we're in business. I print Ayako's leg; her father lends us money; we Makers help downtown survive; Mayor Tiffany wins re-election; Steve keeps his advisory job. I think we've got a deal.

6

TATTOO TIME!

Botticelli meets
San Francisco hippie girls
On my tattoo leg!

I'm so happy for the first time in weeks! Brad Morioka can print me a 3D tattoo leg! My fashion classmates can't wait to see it. Imagine, a tattoo of hippie girls during the City's 1960s Summer of Love inspired by Botticelli. I'm in seventh heaven! I can't wait to wear my new leg. It will beat walking around with a cane, which is so awkward and embarrassing. Soon, I will be the Tattoo Fashion Queen of San Francisco! I'll ask my classmates to post photos on social media so I can show my green fashions and help Brad and his Maker friends with marketing. Hopefully, this will give my mother a reason to stay so I can pursue my dream of bringing the Kansai Look to America. Everybody has seen the Tokyo Street Fashion Look from Harajuku, Shibuya, Yoyogi and Shinjuku, but they have never seen our cool Osaka styles.

Brad moves fast like Osaka business people. Within a week, he has printed out my tattoo leg and comes to my father's office so I can try it on. It's beautiful, with hippie flower patterns flowing down my leg. It is cooler than my San Francisco leggings from the Haight. I wish dad could give me more money for extra legs. I would wear a different tattoo everyday to match my different outfits, but I'm just happy to have one leg. One leg at a time!

I ask Brad to smooth the top edges so it doesn't rub my kneecap. Now my new leg fits perfectly and it's so light. I'm in paradise! It feels funny at first, like I'm walking on air. I'm not used to having it so I limp like a one-legged pirate. Brad encourages me to walk normally. I try and it works. He's so encouraging. I like his chill way of talking. He reminds me of my fashion classmates in the City. So chill, so San Francisco. That's why I love the City. People are chill, even though it's always cold and foggy and the streets are filled with the homeless, trash and poop. They seem to rise above the poop, like Paris, and enjoy the beauty of the City.

After a few days, I feel comfortable walking around town with my tattoo leg. My classmates are shocked. They look at my leg then realize it is hollow and can see through it. What is really cool is that it casts tattoo shadows on the sidewalk so it looks like a Botticelli painting when I wait at intersections. People stare at the shadows then my leg. They ask how it was printed. I give them Brad's business card to help him with marketing. We are the hit of the town. Journalists and bloggers ask for interviews and photos. We agree so we can promote prosthetics and Brad's 3D printing business. And Mayor Tiffany needs all the help she can get. I'm so happy. Instead of feeling sorry for myself, people wish they had cool tattoo legs like me. Some wear tattoo leggings to copy me. That's why the City is so cool. People are open to crazy ideas and cheer you on, not make fun of you like other places. Brad's Maker friends launch the ventures in Kabuki Bank's empty offices so they can stay in town. We're having so much fun that I never want to return to Japan – ghost city or no ghost city. I want to be part of the City's recovery. Daruma time! Down seven times, back up eight. Maybe Brad and his sister Mari will create a tattoo leg series for me. It never hurts to ask.

7

ROBOTVILLE

Bunraku robots
East meets West in puppet land
Do they have spirits?

My 3D tattoo printing business is booming! Thanks to Ayako, I'm bombarded by requests from people ditching their solid prosthetic legs for lighter, see-through tattoo versions. The City is becoming Tattoo City, which has attracted dozens of 3D printer startups and prosthetics companies angling to drum up business and raise venture capital. For me, 3D printing is cool, but it's just a means to my real goal: robots. Now I have a chance to eat, sleep, and breathe robots. That would be a Maker's dream. I want to turn this dead downtown into the coolest Robot City in the world. How can I do it? Japan! Osaka is the robot capital since it's into robotized manufacturing. I should find ways for Makers to invite Japanese robot makers to the City. We could become robot heaven!

My inspiration for robots comes from my dad, who created Bunraku puppets, which are really hand-manipulated robots. As a kid, I wanted to push his ideas into robots. We built Bunraku puppets and Star Wars and Superman robots, mixing ideas from each. My robots had fancy outfits like Bunraku actors. Dad inserted little motors into them so they could walk across the room on their own. Later, we used our TV remote control to navigate them. We had the coolest little robot kingdom in the world, with puppets and robots walking about all over the house. My friends came over to play robot battles in our living room, which looked like a miniature Star Wars movie set. We were living the robot dream.

23

Then dad died and I was left with his Bunraku puppets, lifeless like my robots. It was hard to play with his puppets so I focused on my robots. I remember him recommending that I read "The Buddha in the Robot" by Tokyo University Professor Mori, who said all objects, like stones and robots, have kami – gods – like living creatures. My robots are a way of reincarnating my dad. When I build them, I can hear him chatting with his Bunraku puppets and explaining how they have feelings like us if we listen carefully. At the time, I didn't realize he was describing animism, which Hayao Miyazaki recreated in his animated movies, where everything is alive and magical, full of spirits, like Pinocchio and our Bunraku puppets and robots. My dad's puppets have his spirit so I am never alone, even though it hurts remembering our good times together.

Enough of feeling sorry for myself! I'm a Maker so I build robots. I bring ideas to life. My goal is to make awesome robots with feelings, just like my dad's puppets, so they can help us, not hurt us like killer robots in the movies. I want robots to be our best friends, like R2-D2 and C-3PO. If I can do that, dad would be proud of me. He would smile like he did when I built a cool robot.

Getting back to how to revive the City, we need to get our shit together. We don't have time to sit around moping about gangs, trash and the homeless, but need to do something, anything. But what?

I'm building my latest robot designed like a Kabuki dancer to wow Ayako and her father when the idea strikes me.

Akihabara West! Her father can help the City build Akihabara West! What do I mean by that? Yamaguma-san is a kid like me. He loves robots, toys, anime, manga and gizmos since he grew up near Tokyo's Akihabara district before his father was transferred to Osaka and visited it whenever he was in Tokyo on business. Osaka does not have an Akihabara so he always felt lost, even though Osaka is filled with robot companies. That's why he came to San Francisco. He knows Americans are crazy about J-Pop, Makers, and Star Wars robots so he thought he could start his own little Akihabara in downtown SF, but Covid-19 killed his dreams. His office properties are bleeding money and he cannot get a decent price but he's holding on for a recovery. He's looking for anything that can help him survive financially.

What if he builds Akihabara West? Architects could use VR

to show a cool, next-generation Akihabara to doubters. My friends and I could bring Makers, Burning Man artists, musicians, gamers, AI coders and Metaverse designers. We would start small with a few Maker offices, with mine as the founding startup, and invite others to build critical mass. We just need Yamaguma to seed it. Would he do it? My bet is that he will. He has nothing to lose. Office prices are plummeting and buyers are scarcer than tenants. Downtown is now a huge empty stage for crazies like me who want to build the future, not just sell grass. Mayor Tiffany will promote anything to save downtown and her political skin.

I ask Ayako to speak with her dad, but she says her mother is dead set against staying and wants him to immediately sell his office tower and return to Osaka.

I'm stuck. If he won't help me even after I have created a cool tattoo leg for Ayako, what could work? As Steve Durbin says: Show him the money! If I can show how we can fill his offices, he might be interested. Steve and I have to run the numbers to persuade him. What would work?

I stare at my robots and unsold tattoo legs, contemplating my next moves. There has got to be way. What? Who? How?

I point my controller to my Darth Vader robot, which rolls to me, eyes blinking and speaking in a deep voice: "Follow the Force. Follow the Force…"

8

GOTH CITY

Canyon corridors
Filled with trash and homeless folks
We have hit bottom

Brad is one of the craziest guys I have ever met. Even J-Pop and Gangnam Style fans are not as obsessed as him. He eats and lives robots like my Osaka friends. Why do robots make them so crazy, like little kids? I know they love AstroBoy and Darth Vader but they never grow up, just build bigger robots. Oh well, robot fans are nuts, just like Brad's older sister Mariko who loves Goth leather jackets, jumpsuits and big Harley Davidson motorcycles. They are both crazy. All machines, no classy fashions like their mother's stylish Kyoto kimono fashions. It is no wonder they cannot get along. Competing dreams in the same house -- so American! They're so crazy, but cool, which is why I love San Francisco. You can do whatever you want and not worry about what others think, like in Japan. You can be free and crazy like Brad, Mariko and their mother – crazy in different ways. Dad and I want to be crazy like them, but mom won't let us. She is so Japan.

Maybe we can. Brad asked if my father could create an Akihabara West to revive downtown. He wants to sell his robots with his friends and invite robot makers from Osaka. I think it's a great idea. He is nuts like my father. They are both grown-up kids. My mother says the City will never allow an Akihabara playground downtown, only offices, but the City needs help. Maybe they will listen.

I have an idea! Mariko's Goth fashions could convince dad. He's not into motorcycles but he likes cosplay. Maybe Mari can introduce her Goth designers to my cosplay friends. They could design together. We can invite women designers to bring more people downtown. We can start with tattoo legs for people who want cooler prosthetics. Brad can invite his engineering friends. They can create exoskeletons for paraplegics. Why not? Anything is possible in the City. My father always says: Dream like Americans and soar like Dumbo!

I ask Mari who is excited by my idea. She brings her Goth designer friends to meet my cosplay designers and Brad's 3D printer and exoskeleton engineers at my fashion school. Everyone is excited since they have never met. Brad explains his idea about Akihabara West, Mari's Goth tattoo legs and his exoskeleton legs. It sounds crazy but we like his ideas. Mari has the best idea: she calls it Goth City. That will attract lots of people since she has a big tribe of bikers, tattoo, Goth and motorcycle designers, and hard rock musicians. They can host a Goth Parade. The streets are dark and spooky like canyons – perfect for hard rock music and laser light shows at night. I can wear my cool Goth tattoo legs and LED lights to make the festival acceptable to families. I will ask my father to wear a Japanese tattoo on a bright red happi coat so we can get free PR. We need all the free marketing we can get!

Brad and Mari beg Steve to propose the idea to Mayor Tiffany. We cross our fingers. Supervisors don't like Goth, but our little parade is better than nothing. My cosplay friends design cute Gothette leather dresses for girls and kids and vests with cheerful green and blue wraps so they look innocent. Brad's friends show their cool exoskeletons for paraplegics so we have a good social cause. We nail it. The Berkeley, Marin County and Presidio Heights high society ladies love us and tell their girl friends.

Mayor Tiffany likes our creativity and gives us an OK. We can have our Goth City parade on a quiet weekend when there is nothing happening. It isn't hard since downtown is dead all the time anyway.

Brad builds a Maker Village model in my father's empty storefront on Market Street. It shows everything we will do in Akihabara West: workshops, classes, pop-ups, fashion shows, mini-parades, music concerts, contests, and exhibitions of robots, prosthetics, Goth leathers, motorcycles, electric bikes, cosplay and exoskeletons. Mayor Tiffany asks for a favor: green fashions. It's her hobby and campaign promise. My fashion friends agree so Mayor Tiffany approves our proposal.

We celebrate! We get to realize our dreams. I give my father, Brad and Mari big hugs. We are so excited that we cannot sleep at night. We are back! We are living our dreams! Brad jokes that we have a leg up on others. That's part of our advertising campaign. My tattoo leg will be famous. It will be the longest, coolest, and sexiest tattoo leg in the world! My dad loves it. My mom is not amused.

9

MAKER VILLAGE

Robots and cosplay
Like puppets sprawled on the street
We invent futures

I am so jazzed by Mayor Tiffany's approval of our Goth City concept that I cannot sleep and focus on my schoolwork. All I want to do all day is build robots, e-bikes, prosthetics and exoskeletons until I collapse. But I don't care. School is always there; the City needs our help now or we don't have future careers here. I still have Alan Kay's immortal words 3D printed onto my desk plaque: The best way to predict the future is to invent it. I'm an inventor; I'm a Maker; I invent futures for all of us. Now is the time for my Maker buddies and me to show the world what's possible. It's better than just creating sci-fi graphic novels, games and movies. We are building real things that you can touch, feel and smell. We are reinventing our dead downtown from scratch. We will 3D print it into existence. I'm inviting all frustrated Makers around the world to join us. How cool is that? The City gave us a blank slate with blank minds in power so we'll show them how creativity and inventors can change and improve the world.

　　　Yamaguchi-san is a messenger from heaven. He provides free office space and pop-up stores on Market Street so everyone can drop in and see our demos and exhibits. We post all over social media and thousands of kids and their parents show up. Weekends are crazy since so many people jump off BART and pack our pop-ups, buying everything in sight. That's what we love about robot, Goth, sci-fi and cosplay fans; they buy anything cool. My Maker dream is coming true! Within weeks, our pop-up shops are open from morning till late night so Makers, Goth, biker and coplay designers want to open their offices with us. Yamaguchi-san grins and high-fives everyone pouring into our shops. He rediscovers his inner kid. He wears a Japanese bozoku black weather jacket and jumpsuit with aviator glasses to look like a James Dean biker and models for bloggers and journalists who swarm all over our little Maker Village. He is a master of free marketing. "Kabuki Magic!", "Goth Banker Goes Cosplay!", and "Tattoo Legs Galore!". We get so much global coverage that we are all famous overnight. SF is on fire!

Mayor Tiffany is absolutely thrilled by our huge success on a mini-budget with no City funding involved at all. All we need is cheap space and talent. She stands before television cameras proudly describing our strategy.

"In San Francisco, we turn lemons into tasty lemonade for our families and friends. People say it's over for the City, but they have not studied our history. After the 1906 and 1989 earthquakes and the 1973, 1980, 1990, 2000, 2008 and 2020 market crashes, we did not lie down and play dead. We bounced back with fresh ideas and talent. We are inventors; we are designers; we are artists; we are creators. We transform ugliness, disasters and poverty into beauty, happiness and joy. That is who we are. We are Makers!"

I couldn't have said it better or more eloquently myself. Now that we have Mayor Tiffany on our side, it is show time for the big rollout: Akihabara West!

10

AKIHABARA WEST

Robots and e-bikes
Exoskeletons, oh my!
What has Japan wrought?

Brad is a magician. He turns everything miserable into gold. He replaced my stump leg with a beautiful tattoo leg. He encouraged my father to stay and fund his Maker friends. He got Mariko to invite her Goth designers and bikers to reinvent downtown. He invited my cosplay fashion friends to join Mari and Mayor Tiffany's green fashion designers. He invited his Maker friends who brought their 3D printers, robots, e-bikes, exoskeletons and prosthetics designers to create the world's first Goth City center. Now he begs my father to open up his dream project: Akihabara West.

For decades, my father was a frustrated banker wishing he could be a designer like Brad but family and work took over. He had to run our family's bank, which opened two hundred years ago. He wanted to run away to San Francisco, but his father never let him leave. My father begged to have my uncle run our Osaka headquarter so he could open a San Francisco branch. My family criticized him as irresponsible, but he didn't care. He wanted to escape and pursue the American Dream that he saw in Hollywood movies. When I was a child, I would watch him gazing out the window to America far away across the sea, wishing he were in California and pursuing his secret dream -- building Akihabara West – like Walt Disney did with Disneyland. He bought books about Disney and studied them religiously. He studied theme parks, architecture, urban design, construction and VR. He imagined himself a Japanese Disney bringing cool Akihabara vibes to America, like Akio Morita did with

Sony and Nintendo with Pokemon. But reality kept us trapped in Osaka. I watched him age, seeing his sadness as his dream vanished over the years. He was always depressed and drank heavily. He and my mother always argued. I felt badly for him and wanted to help, but my mother insisted that he pay more attention to the bank after the huge 2019 typhoon flooded Osaka. But he still dreamed about California, fed up with Osaka's weak recovery, and ignored her. He opened Kabuki Bank in San Francisco, just in time for the Covid-19 shutdown, the worst possible time. Mother wanted him to shut the office and return to Osaka, but he would not. He sold some large offices at a loss to keep a few small offices open. He said the pandemic would end and companies would need our little bank to survive and recover. He was right; many small businesses are asking my father for loans.

"We cannot leave now," says father. "The City needs us. Small shops need us. We cannot quit."

"But mother is upset," I say.

"Let her visit Osaka. We can stay since Mari's Goth City and Brad's Maker Village idea are working. We can leverage them to build Akihabara West."

"You're actually going to build it?"

"Why not? You only live once. I need to try now or I will always regret it. Disney and Akio Morita didn't quit during tough times. They kept their vision and gave it their all. I will never give up. I know Americans want Akihabara West. They need it as much as San Francisco, but the City just doesn't realize it. We need to show them."

My father's eyes light up like a child waiting for Christmas. I knew he was a dreamer, but I have never seen him so excited in my life. He cannot sleep and talks about Akihabara West all day. My mother threatens to leave. Dad shrugs and keeps talking about Akihabara West. I let him since I want to stay and design cool street fashion, like Tokyo fashionistas, but better. We are crazy like Brad, Mariko, Yumiko and their mother. We have become crazy San Franciscans.

My father wastes no time. He hires graphic designers to create Akihabara West logos and virtual models for our marketing campaign. Soon, our boring bank office turns into a lively, colorful studio filled with sketches, storyboards, models and VR models.

Akihabara West is a mix of Akihabara, with its big signs, high-rises, gaudy electronics shops, and neon lights, and Disneyland, with its characters, parades, music, costumes and fireworks. It is our Japanese Disneyland.

Mayor Tiffany, Brad, Mari and their friends are stunned. They have never seen anything like it in the Bay Area. Akihabara West makes Chinatown, Mission and the Haight look dull. Bay Area folks and tourists agree and storm our website. They cannot wait for it to open with a big parade.

My father shows his masterpiece to the board of supervisors who file through our studio like school children on tour. Their eyes roll as he waves his hands about like Walt Disney and explains how he plans to bring in major Japanese and Asian electronics companies, animation studios, retailers and event organizers. They are skeptical, but have nothing better in mind so they nod their approval. Mayor Tiffany wears her famous green campaign gown to promote her Green Fashion initiative. The media eats it up, especially Japanese television stations and bloggers. They call my father the "Shohei Ohtani of Urban Entertainment."

Soon, our faces appear all over Japan and the world like Munchkins led by my father, who the western press calls "The Wizard of San Francisco," with his fairy godmother, Mayor Tiffany, dressed in her famous green gowns. My father, Mayor Tiffany, and the city supervisors crack open a sake barrel with mallets to christen our playground. We are in business! In less than a few months, my father has achieved his childhood dream. He is so happy that he hugs everyone again and again like a child – not very Japanese at all – but then we're in SF. My mother is embarrassed; she married a kid. But that's OK with me. I want a kid as my father. He is definitely more fun and interesting than most Japanese fathers who are boring company men, in fact, almost all fathers. He is the best father a girl could ever have!

Akihabara West launches with a big parade on Market Street, led by Mayor Tiffany in her green gown and crown, and my father, wearing his samurai Goth helmet and armor, just like Shohei after he hits a home run. I march behind them, proudly showing my tattoo leg, along with my friends who show off their tattoo legs. We are the Tattoo City team. Mariko leads her Goth City team. Brad leads his Maker Village team on a float with robots and exoskeletons. Emiko leads her Cosplay team and her mother the Kyoto Kimono Minds fashion design team. We have so many fans wearing their own designs that our little parade lasts for one hour.

Akihabara West attracts thousands of visitors everyday. Sightseers, school children, families, foreign tour groups, educators, journalists, city officials and others swamp our pop-up shops and offices, asking questions and wondering how they can create their own Maker villages downtown. Many kids and even adults wear J-Pop outfits and green gowns. Mayor Tiffany, Brad and my father give advice like sports coaches to visitors who line up to take photos with us in front of my father's shop. We are rolling and we are hot!

Part 2

The Paradise

11

SAN FRANCISCO ROCKS!

Gold miners galore
Crowding into our ghost town
Another Gold Rush!

San Francisco has always attracted gold miners seeking their mother lode. Even my mother, a Kyoto kimono designer, arrived with her classy kimonos, dreaming of fame and fortune. Boom is our brand, like Levi jeans, overpriced food and sourdough. We go from boom to bust, again and again, like a Daruma doll. It has happened so many times that people lose track, as Mayor Tiffany reminds us: 1849, 1880s, 1906, 1941, 1950, 1967, 1994, 2000, 2008, 2020 and today. It becomes her mantra to educate the media and skeptics. Each time we enjoy a Gold Rush rocket ride then collapse into a deep slump. The media always pronounces us dead and red states cheer, then we invent the Next New Thing, boom again and red states copy us and recruit our companies. Newspapers love us; they make a fortune on ads from our booms and busts.

Now we are entering my fourth boom. I can feel it in my bones. But this one is harder since things are so expensive. Condos start at a million dollars; homes at two million. Who has that kind of money? Definitely not the average family. Steve is spot on: "San Francisco used to be old and poor in the 1930s, young and poor in the 1960s, young and rich since the 1990s, and now old and rich." You need to be a baby boomer who bought a rundown home in the 1980s or a corporation to afford anything around here. Downtown is a playground for big developers, landowners and corporations. There is no place for little guys like us.

How can we survive? We do gig jobs for minimum wages and live with our parents or guys in "man camps." We get great tech jobs during booms but are jettisoned during slumps. We don't see a future anywhere in the Bay Area so most of my friends have moved to Sacramento, Reno and Texas. They hate it but they have no choice. We are a Lost Generation who can't afford to live here unless our parents bought homes decades ago or the City figures out how to build small, affordable housing, then my friends would come rushing back in a flash to enjoy our foods, fog, vibes and friends. But that's a "Full House" fantasy, like owning a spiffy Victorian.

There's always hope. Angel investors and VCs are rushing into generative AI (GenAI) like the dot.com madness long ago. They forget our past crashes and are investing heavily into anything called AI so entrepreneurs put AI into their marketing and investor pitches. A few years ago, it was Metaverse this, Metaverse that, then blockchain, crypto currencies, and NFTs (non-fungible tokens). Now it's AI for everything, everywhere, all at once. Even Mayor Tiffany has AI fever, declaring us the "AI Capital." It is Chaplin's "Gold Rush" again with techies rushing into the City to raise venture capital and strike the mother lode. How pathetic! How San Francisco!

I laugh with my mother and sisters who think techies are crazy, but they have their own dreams of hitting it big with their fashion brands: Kimonos, Goth, Cosplay and Virtual. They are planning to use AI like everyone else in this crazy town. We're all inhaling and we don't even need grass to get high. It's in the air.

The Gold Rush virus has infected Ayako's tattoo leg friends and her father. They rush about recruiting entrepreneurs and investors and hosting parties, with Ayako's fashion models parading down makeshift runways to make things interesting and attract the guys. It works. Downtown is waking up. What used to be blocks and blocks of empty streets and buildings is transforming before our eyes. Office lights are on late at night. GenAI coders are pouring into the City to find their "product-market fit," as we used to call marketing and sales. They aim to raise venture capital, grow fast globally, go public then buy their mansions in Pacific Heights above us folks in Japantown. It's so familiar and depressing. Developers breathe down our necks to "revitalize" Japantown by bulldozing us out of town and putting up luxury resorts for their new rich tech clients.

Man, I hate it. We are the problem, all of us who want to

stay in the City. We all dream of finding great jobs but then become the new gold miners pushing out the natives. I'm emotionally split. I'm a Maker, but I don't want to bulldoze my friends into oblivion. There is something as urban justice. Ah, the Barbary Coast strikes again.

My sisters and friends aren't the only dreamers. Mayor Tiffany and Steve want a booming downtown too, but without gentrification, evictions and homelessness. The City promotes "San Francisco Rocks!" but our families and the poor are the ones being pushed out. It's a no-win scenario. No investments, no jobs and no money, but too many jobs and evictions boom. The City loses either way. Are we stuck in a perpetual Catch 22, a SF Noir nightmare? Is there no way out of this curse?

Steve and I hunker down with Yamaguma-san to see how we can keep young people in the City. My idea is to create cheap co-working and co-living spaces where entrepreneurs like my sisters and me can open our tiny startups. We don't need fancy digs, just simple capsule bedrooms, since we work most of the time in our studios and labs.

Yamaguma-san agrees. He thinks the City should think like Japan. Capsule living spaces could work in his offices, which now waste too much space, so he hires a top Tokyo capsule hotel designer to redesign it for co-working/living spaces. The designer is a hip young woman, Ai Nakano, who graduated from Keio University in architecture and interior design. She is a friend of Yoko Hamabe, the solar sculpture designer who the City hires for many of its public places. Together, they trick out Kabuki Bank's offices and turn them into a Japanese village with tiny, rounded capsules, open kitchens, and joint bathrooms, steam rooms and hot baths. The places are simple, but elegant and tasteful, with miniature rock gardens and organic plants along the windows. To set the mood, they pump in soothing nature sounds and birdcalls recorded along the coast. It's like walking along the Marin Headlands.

Our launch parties are awesome. Ayako, Yoko and Ai invite their music, fashion and art friends to create Akihabara West demos, pop-up shops and VR screens on the ground floor. With the lights turned down, the lobbies and side gardens look like a cross between Akihabara and Kyoto gardens, with cool J-Pop, K-Pop and Bay Area music playing from stereo speakers. It's a techno-artist's paradise.

Thousands of kids attend our parties, celebrating the revival of Kabuki Bank's properties. San Francisco Rocks! We have a chance to survive and thrive during the coming GenAI and Metaverse boom!

12

COSPLAY CITY

Bring in the women
Tricked out in cosplay fashions
The City survives!

My father and Brad get along so well that they are like father and son. In truth, my father always wanted a son and Brad misses his father, so it's a perfect match. But they are tech heads dreaming of robots, video games, home gadgets and gizmos so they attract mostly guys. We girls feel left out so Emiko and I organize cosplay parties, fashion shows and contests to bring out women. It works like magic and attracts guys since Bay Area folks love to dress up for Halloween, parties, street festivals and parades. They are like little kids. The Star Wars and Star Trek fans are the wildest, wearing every possible costume from the series. Mari and I bring out the Goth crowd who wear tattoos everywhere. My new friends wear hip tattoo prosthetic legs so we look like fancier versions of Brad's exoskeleton fans.

Our big rollout is the Cherry Blossom Festival parade, which starts at city hall and winds through downtown to Japantown. But this year, the parade starts on Thursday evening and goes down Market Street past the pop-up exhibits in Akihabara West on Thursday, Friday and Saturday so we can party until late into the night. Bay Area folks love to party so our Cosplay Parade attracts tens of thousands of young people and their families who dress up and join our parade. Downtown looks like "Disneyland North" with cosplayers wearing outfits of all different types: African princesses, Asian kings and queens, Martians, gold miners, French countesses, Brazilian samba dancers, Filipino stick dancers, Mongolian horse riders, and Argentinian cowboys. Mayor Tiffany loves our parade since she wants to create a "UN of Green Fashion." Cosplay gives her an easy way to kickstart her campaign to revive downtown. We ask everyone to wear recycled clothes so poor families can join in. No need to show wealth, just pure creativity! The Black, LatinX and Asian kids love it since they can create their own styles to look cool. Mayor Tiffany calls it the new "San Francisco Look."

Akihabara West and our Cosplay Parade appear on nearly every news channel, fashion blog, and travel guide. Except for security, the City has jumpstarted its downtown recovery with sponsors so my father is a hero. Photographers rush to take photos of him in his Goth samurai helmet and armor and me wearing my tattoo leg, which started the whole thing, with Brad shaking hands with my father in front of our Kabuki Bank logo. "Shohei Banker!," "Cosplay SF!", "Akihabara West Playland!", and "I Left My Dollars in San Francisco." Mayor Tiffany and my father are laughing all the way to his bank.

13

AI GOLD RUSH

AI in thar hills!
Gold miners flood the City
Six-dollar croissants

A new Gold Rush of AI and regenerative fashion is here. Makers, coders and entertainers struggling from tech layoffs and recession, joined by armies of jobless baby boomers, Millennials and Gen Z, scramble for the brass ring to lift themselves out of poverty and gain fame and fortune. I'm the rare bird from Japantown, which misses these booms since we focus on culture and local matters, not tech like our Chinese, Koreans, Indians, Filipinos and Vietnamese classmates. We Japanese Americans are missing in action; I'm usually the only one at Maker events. My sisters make rare sightings of our Japantown friends at Goth, Cosplay and VR events, but they look like a lost battalion in the heat of battle. Japantown lives in its golden past while Akihabara West is shaking it up with the City's future. Now it's cool to be a Japanese geek, a Shohei tech power hitter. My new Osaka friends are creating wild manga, anime and cosplay fashions so I feel right at home, especially when robot makers show up. Like mom, I'm a Kansai fan at heart.

Generative AI trumps it all. Once the plaything of techies, it has gone viral to every company. Mayor Tiffany plays up our new title as "AI Capital of the World." A new wave of startups, tech giants, old companies and investors is flooding downtown. Founders are pitching venture capitalists like the 2010s to expand into the U.S. market. The good old days are here, chirps Mayor Tiffany like a proud mother. She wears green gowns at City events to promote regenerative fashion so women feel comfortable in this tech boom.

"We're not going to be Bro City again like Silicon Valley," she declares. "We will be open and equal. Women will drive our cultural Renaissance."

Is she smoking pot? Steve said she was a pot-smoking bro in high school before she became a Navy fighter pilot. I still can't believe she morphed from a Mission bro gamer to a "Top Gun" Navy pilot, Stanford data jock and now a green fashionista. Talk about political chameleon. Now she wants to show that it's possible for poor kids to escape poverty through education and tech. She sees Akihabara West as a catalyst to save downtown and their future careers led by Asian education grinds.

My AI bros love Mayor Tiff who understands their jargon about algorithms, data sets, machine learning, inference and the other arcane terminology. She loves talking shop instead of battling with old-fashioned Luddite supervisors who have absolutely no clue about tech and us young people. She is raising a seed fund from private investors and foundations for racial and gender inclusion and planning "AI Top Gun" challenges. AI is our new lottery so she's doubling down.

To launch our "AI Capital" program, Mayor Tiffany surrounds herself with the top guns from tech giants, VCs, angel investors, Cal and Stanford professors, and K-12 STEAM educators. The stage is so crowded with talent that there's not enough space for their egos. But Mayor Tiffany smiles; they hold the secret formulas to our future. The City has no choice: Tech or Bust! Progressives and old-timers may hate tech and prefer the arts, but tech is the future of America and the world. It is already driving Hollywood and the arts. SF needs billions of dollars of income and taxes to cover our nearly billion-dollar budget deficit in the coming years or we face big layoffs. Without a tech revival, Mayor Tiff knows she and the City have no political or financial future, so she is jettisoning all fears and plunging ahead. To calm the critics, she is recruiting sponsors for her Regenerative Fashion program to promote the arts, design, humanities and women. Our fashion industry will be green, smart and super cool.

Her "AI Rocks!" program rolls out smoothly like jets on a flight deck. All hands are on deck – every City agency, corporate sponsor and educator – who are prepared for our "Greatest AI Show on Earth" worthy of Cecile B. De Mille and George Lucas who

43

attends incognito, wearing a cheap-looking hat and sunglasses to avoid detection by swarms of Jedi fans.

Mayor Tiffany opens the press conference with an amazing GenAI movie trailer showing a futuristic San Francisco in 2030 that looks like a Virtual Hollywood on steroids, created by Pixar and LucasFilm storytellers.

"Like Pinocchio," she declares. "I want "prompt engineers" to become our new puppeteers who can manage AI puppets for public, educational, and environmental purposes. We will control AI, not let it controls us. We want AI for good!"

Huge applause. Mayor Tiffany describes our future SF filled with Black, LatinX, Asian, indigenous, white and other groups who wear modernistic costumes of their cultures, like Wakanda, but their avatars are not just dancing and fighting. They are building floating cities and permaculture gardens, wearing trippy green fashions, and preparing great feasts of international dishes. Her vision is a foodie fashion, music and art paradise filled with a calendar chock full of street fairs, cultural events, parades, music concerts, and dance performances. She invites the Giants, Warriors and 49ers to demo their virtual games, as well as legions of Star Wars and Star Trek spaceships and drones circling the City like the Blue Angels during Fleet Week. It's a VR meets AI Metaverse paradise in spades – with robots!

Everyone is stunned. We have never seen such a massive display of advanced AI for healing purposes. Mayor Tiffany jokes that it's her "shock and awe" strategy to wake up the City. After years of pandemic, layoffs, recession and media criticism, her vision comes as a breath of fresh air, especially to graduates who have given up hope of ever finding jobs in their field. For my Ohlone, Black, Latino, and Asian classmates, it's much deeper – centuries of slavery, genocide, hostility, redlining and exclusion – so they remain skeptical, even though she's a woman of color.

"We are San Francisco!" Mayor Tiffany shouts to cheering audiences around the world. "We never surrender to adversity. We stand up, proud and strong, and work hard to rebuild our lives and help our families and friends around the world. We are the future! I want you to join us and create the next phase of human evolution. We want wisdom AI with compassion and caring. That is why we are called San Francisco, after Saint Francis of Assisi, not Robot City (ouch!). We are not robots; we are free humans with free will and political freedoms. That is why I joined the Navy, why we oppose tyrants around the world and why the City supports redress – so every San Franciscan has hope and a chance for a better future. Together, we will work together to achieve our goal: a More Perfect City."

Again stunned silence. Is she high on something? We have never heard Mayor Tiffany declare her deepest beliefs. We always saw her as a Mission game bro, Navy Top Gun and Stanford data jock focused on business and tech, never as a human with a big heart who grew up poor with her abandoned mother in the Mission, which left deep scars that Steve says she can never forget.

With that unforgettable kickoff speech, the City transforms overnight into a new world, as if Tinker Bell has sprinkled pixie dust on our sleeping town. With a few words, Mayor Tiff has energized us. We are hopeful and transformed from puppets mesmerized by our phones into breathing, feeling people who care about each other and something bigger than themselves. At least that's her game plan.

Steve says that's why she ran for mayor. She wants to play the biggest game on the biggest stage before the global media – reinventing downtown -- a real game with real lives and real business. Steve calls it our Summer of Love 2.0 "Hail Mary" pass into the end zone.

14

LITTLE OSAKA

Kansai fever strikes
Kabuki robots, oh my!
Friends descend on us

Mayor Tiffany is amazing. Her speech kicked off excitement in
Osaka, which lost contact with SF during political controversies.
Like long-lost cousins, we are reconnecting on a business and J-Pop
level, thanks to my father and Mrs. Morioka's Kyoto kimono
designers. Suddenly, Osaka is hot again. Brad and my father invite
hundreds of Osaka robot makers to open shop in Akihabara West,
which they do, one after another, initially afraid of the Tenderloin
crime, but gradually reassured by opening near MOMA. They create
their own district called "Little Osaka" and put up neon signs to
make it look like downtown Osaka. Soon, tourists come to see our
SF version. They buy Hanshin Tigers baseball caps as well as SF
Giants jackets. Fans want to see the Tigers play the Giants at Oracle
Park, which Mayor Tiffany is negotiating with the Osaka mayor.
Baseball fans are going nuts. For the first time in years, my parents
are cheering for the Tigers. We cannot wait to see them. Who
knows? Maybe one of their players will be the next Shohei Ohtani.

      The real surprise is the robot makers. They arrive like Star
Wars troopers wearing Astro Boy and other J-Pop characters, along
with the cosplay fans that Emi and I invited. Their robots roll into
Little Osaka in a parade that attracts sci-fi fans who love the blinking,
talking robots that jump about, make martial arts moves, and dance
to J-Pop, hip-hop and rap music. Brad and my father cheer like little
boys. Emi and I cheer like little girls. We are so happy after being

made fun of. I have finally found my tribe!

Mayor Tiffany leads the parade with the Osaka mayor who wears a beautiful green kimono designed by Mrs. Morioka. They join a float with a dozen beautiful women wearing green kimonos of all different patterns and shades. I have never seen kimonos with recycled textiles. That is a first for the City.

My biggest thrill is riding the float with my tattoo team. We asked Brad's Maker bros to 3D print see-through tattoo legs. Their designs are gorgeous. We are the hit of the parade. Attendees post videos online so we are famous worldwide. The biggest cheers come when the Army float with veterans showing off their printed tattoo arms and legs. Their designs make us ours look tame. They have tattoos of wild tigers, lions and bears, oh my, and scorpions, boa constrictors, dinosaurs and panthers. Their cool designs go viral. Their banner – Tattoo Vets! – grabs the headlines.

The real fun begins when my father launches a Robot Kingdom contest to promote Little Osaka. Overnight, our Kabuki Bank website is filled with hundreds of cool robot designs from around the world. My father asks an online retailer to sell them and shows the top robots in the Little Osaka exhibition hall on Market Street. Within a week hundreds of robots arrive and thousands of fans line up to see them. The best displays are dancing robots, especially dancing robots that move like real Kabuki actors. My father is over the moon! He picks the top Kabuki robots that will be logos for our bank.

Brad goes crazy making robots and taking 3D printing orders for robot parts. Soon, his little Kansai Robots shop is flooded with fans and customers who order everything that he and his buddies can print. We are so proud of him. His Akihabara West idea helped save my father's bank. Now he can stay by printing his dream robots. My tattoo leg business is also growing, thanks to my friends and the veterans. We are thinking of creating Tattoo City, but that will have to wait. I need to find friends who can since we don't want people only interested in money, but people who want to help paraplegics, veterans and our friends.

So Little Osaka gets off to a great start. My father, Brad and our team are so happy. Only in SF! It would take us years to do the same in Osaka so I'm glad my father insisted on staying here. He always admired Disney and Lucas for their vision and wanted to create his own "Disneyland for Adults" in SF. For decades, it was only a dream. Our friends made fun of him. Now they are envious. While they work at boring jobs, he is pursing his American Dream. He is the adult kid he always wanted to be, but was afraid to show in public. He is creating his own Disneyland – our Little Osaka – that he can proudly show the world. At night, sitting alone at his workbench, he uses GenAI to create images of a bigger, amazing futuristic Little Osaka and Akihabara West. They look like Solar Punk fantasies in manga cartoons that he loves, but he wants to turn them into reality. He wants to become the "Japanese Disney."

15

SOUL CITY

Glitter and bangles
Magic fairies and dragons
Osaka Punk lives!

Yamaguma-san creates his childhood dream: Little Osaka filled with
Osaka Punk characters, scenes and stories based on Kansai myths.
Like a madman, he works late into the night using GenAI creating
hundreds of images for his futuristic Little Osaka, inspired by
Disneyland and Disney World, which he spends hours on, building
everything in detail. He is a hardcore perfectionist. Ayako says he is
a frustrated designer and inventor who only opened Kabuki Bank to
finance his hobbies and buddies. Now he can finally realize his
dreams in the ultimate Nerd City: San Francisco.

Little Osaka emerges like a glittering, neon-lit swan in a dark,
forbidding downtown filled with the homeless, trash and gangs. It
looks like a magical Disneyland dropped into a depressing Hollywood
dystopia. Nobody comes downtown, except to our little Akihabara
West and Little Osaka. The rest of downtown is still ghostly silent.
Yamaguma-san, Mayor Tiffany, Steve and I want to change that.
They want to transform downtown into a shining "Disneyland for
Adults." Like Yamaguma-san, she's a closet Disney fan. She plays
Star Wars games at night when she's not busy with city matters.

"We have nothing to lose," she tells Yamaguma-san and me.
"Tech giants are avoiding us. GenAI founders and investors love us.
Foreigners are pouring into our co-working/co-living space to raise
VC funding. We are becoming the "AI Capital" and, thankfully, the
3D Metaverse is coming, thanks to the big boys in Asia and Silicon

Valley. If we play it right, the City will be "Digital Hollywood." We might as well shoot for the moon since there's no Superman to rescue us."

Our Superman is Yamaguma-san who claims he can bring Astro Boy, Godzilla and Osaka robots. He has the right industry connections in Osaka so we sit down with him, Mayor Tiffany, Steve and her team to discuss how to build our "Disneyland for Adults."

"First of all," says Mayor Tiffany. "It must be safe, clean and convenient for children and families, just like Disneyland. They must be treated like guests by all of us. Our homeless hosts will be given food, housing, green uniforms and training to welcome everyone with pride. Our LGBT+ pride must be broadened to civic pride for all of us. We must rock."

"With rock festivals!" says Steve. "I can bring my bros in the Fillmore who know everyone in the music scene."

"Summer of Love 2.0!" I add. "I missed the 1960s so I want to see the real thing in VR."

"Done!" says Mayor Tiffany. "Instead of Philip Souza, we'll ask Santana, the Grateful Dead and the Doors to kick off our Virtual Haight."

"Hippie Land?" I ask.

"Way cooler," says Steve. "Soul City!"

"Sounds only Fillmore to me."

"Soul is universal. This is the City of Love, with our UN heritage. We should honor it but make it cooler and relevant. Not just pious, high-sounding shit, but down home soul music, like the 1960s, with the blues, hippie music and R&B."

"Hippie music? You mean rock music. Santana wasn't a hippie. He's a bro from the hood. And my Japantown bros play rap with Fillmore bros, so what's the problem? We're all soul brothers."

"Brad has a point," says Mayor Tiffany. "We are all soul brothers and sisters joined at the hip, not just hippies, so we should celebrate our roots and connections in music. All kinds of music – wild, weird, rock, Latin, R&D, hip hop, rap, blues, Indian, Thai, J-Pop, C-Pop -- whatever people want to hear. Don't forget, we are San Francisco cool."

We sit back, dazed. Is that the real Mayor Tiffany reappearing after all these decades? She has not lost her jive and soul from the Mission. We are reassured. She's still the real thing.

"Then Soul City it is!" We chime in.

Soul City definitely sounds more fun and SF than "Disneyland for Adults," which is a put-down by outsiders. So we go with it: Soul City!"

Tiff punches her fists into the air.

"All for one and one for all," she yells. "This is for our kids and families!"

In true San Francisco style, we launch one of the coolest Soul City music festivals ever seen. Steve leverages Virtual Fillmore nightclubs and dance halls to kick off the festival with his Afro-Latino jazz and reggae bands. Carlos Montoya invites his Native rock buddies, Rafael Molina-Tanaka his Latin, salsa, and mariachi blues brothers. I invite the Asian rockers who play cool mixes of Indonesian, Korean, Tibetan, Filipino, Japanese and Indian music. Before we know it, our Soul City site is filled with hundreds of Bay Area rock groups. Tiff's bros invite hundreds of local dance troupes that bring color, romance, women and their admirers. Soon, the entire Bay Area is rocking and rolling to fusion rock bands and dancing to the rhythms of the dance troupes in classrooms and living rooms around the world.

"We are the Soul City rock capital of the world!" shouts Tiff, her fists pumped overhead like Rocky. "Summer of Love 2.0, we have arrived!"

To celebrate our collective achievement, Tiff lights up city hall with multicolor LED screens and light drones that display our fusion music rockers in 3D, complete with their music blaring over Civic Center Plaza where hundreds of kids and their families dance to the tunes everyday at 5pm and every weekend. The downtown merchants, struggling since Covid-19 hit, love us and fill their shops with Soul City posters, T-shirts, mugs, coffee holders and caps. The tax revenues pour into the City's coffers. Mayor Tiffany makes sure to allocate a healthy chunk to temporary shelters and permanent housing for the homeless.

Tiff reminds us: A ghost city is too good a disaster to waste.

16

COSPLAY CITY

J-Pop rappers all
Dressed in cosplay finery
Kansai has arrived!

Major Tiffany, my father, Brad, Steve and their friends are having all the fun with their rock friends, but we women feel left out. Why can't we "own" downtown like the guys? So I ask Mari, Emi, and Yumi for their ideas. How can we girls create our own fun districts in Little Osaka?

"First of all, we need fashion," says Mari. "I'll bring in my Goth designers. They'll dress in faux leather."

"Faux leather?" I ask. "What's that?"

"No animal skins. We're against killing and only use recycled plastics."

"Can you design them for my tattoo fans?"

"Anything you want. We can design tattoo fabrics and jewelry. Do you have a cool theme?"

I sit back and think hard. I have never been asked by anyone for my ideas, just told what to do. Mari is really different.

"What about a J-Pop Festival? Emi and I can invite all of our friends and fans."

"Too common and imported. We need something uniquely San Francisco."

Emi and I brainstorm more ideas. I'm not used to brainstorming like Americans. In Japan, we work as teams, but don't make up things on demand. It has to fit into traditions. Americans call it groupthink, but it works for us.

"What about a Green Cosplay fashion show?" asks Emi. "We can design everything with recycled materials. Mayor Tiffany is promoting the idea so we can get her support."

"That works. I'll get my designers to create a Faux Live! Exhibition so people can see how we e-bikers recycle materials."

"E-bikers! My father can invite Japanese e-bike makers! Can you make cool faux leather jackets for them? With club decals?"

"Anything you want. This is going to be fun. Imagine, punk e-bikers parading down Market Street. That ought to grab the media. I always thought Japanese were always so staid. Not fun like my wild Japanese e-biker friends."

"We're not all square. Emi's cosplay friends ride e-scooters and e-bikes."

"Then let's create a cool Cosplay City and invite everyone, including non-bikers and non-Goth folks. Cosplay is perfect since it will probably attract Star Wars, Star Trek and Comicon fans who will attract new fans."

One thing I like about Mari is that she so open and different. First, she helped me design cool tattoo legs for my friends. Now she offers cool faux leather for Emi's cosplay friends. Soon we'll have the biggest green cosplay center in the world! My father and I could never imagine it by ourselves.

Within weeks, Mari rallies her Goth designers. Emi gathers her cosplay friends. I invite my tattoo fans. We meet at co-working/co-living spaces my father provides free to attract renters and sponsors. Mari's idea works. Soon, our spaces are filled with Goth, tattoo, cosplay and green fashion designers. It's the first time ever. Bloggers post cool photos and videos so we are packed with designers. My father's dream has come true! Kabuki Bank has launched an "American Kabuki" movement of designers in our Little Osaka. We should sell T-shirts. The Osaka mayor is so proud of us that she comes with a huge group and gives my father an honorary "Citizen of Osaka" medal. I get a Little Osaka tattoo leg version.

I'm so happy for the first time since I lost my leg! My mother hugs my father and me and apologies for insisting on returning to Osaka. She says her Osaka friends now want to join us, especially their kids who are bored with school and gig jobs.

Emi and I invite cosplayers to show their green fashions. Mari's e-biker friends wear green faux leather jackets and jumpsuits.

Mayor Tiffany wears her world-famous green gown with a tattoo print and faux leather sun hat. She auctions it off to raise money for my friends who cannot afford a tattoo leg. I am walking on air with delight! Everyone loves my tattoo leg so I asked my father if he would buy more from Brad. He agrees so I give him a big hug. I love his crazy Kabuki vision and hope it helps the City revive. At least we are having fun – SF style.

17

C-POP CITY

Chinese own the town
From Chinatown to Sunset
The new Gold Mountain!

Our American Kabuki movement is cool, but Japanese Americans are a tiny island in a sea of black hair. When I was a kid, Chinese Americans ran "Gold Mountain," which stretched from Chinatown on Grant Avenue on the east side to the outer Richmond and Sunset on the west side. Even though the City has become a hot pot of Asian American Pacific Island (AAPI) newcomers, the Chinese still rule.

A classic example is Bill Ting, a Cal grad and rival mayoral candidate, who created C-Pop City to outshine our tiny Little Osaka. He brings financial firepower to the City, which welcomes his dollars, but it's unfair competition. He brings deep pockets from Chinese expatriates and offshore corporations around the world that could easily invest hundreds of billions to expand Chinatown into the Financial District and South of Market (SOMA) to create one huge "Gold Mountain." Bill signals his "Greater China" strategy by establishing a China Bank near Kabuki Bank and flies dozens of Asian flags of nations with expat Chinese communities to attract supporters. We're playing simple chess; he's playing go and even labels his initiative "Go, China SF!"

A red alert goes up in city hall. Although Mayor Tiffany welcomes Bill's investor friends, federal agencies warn her so she wants to control their influence by establishing a City-run bank that

55

gives first priority to local small businesses. No dummy LLC corporate shells for her taste. She brings in American banks and Silicon Valley's financial tech boys to create a Crypto Market Street on blockchain that will provide crypto financing using digital coins, crowdfunding, green bonds, NFTs (non-fungible tokens), and other crypto coupons printed by the City. I'm not a financial whiz, but Steve, Yamaguma-san and Mayor Tiffany are teaching me a hell of a lot about finance.

"We will be the Crypto Bank capital of the world," she declares, announcing the City's public bank. The shock waves around the world are huge. Overnight, thousands of foreign and U.S. funds, investors and companies set up accounts to avoid missing the action and are watching Mayor Tiffany under a microscope. FOMO (Fear of Missing Out) reigns supreme.

Mayor Tiffany is overjoyed, but Yamaguma-san is terrified since Bill's China Bank and Mayor Tiffany's Crypto Street bank could grab all of the business and buy up downtown so he has to move faster. He calls his Tokyo and Osaka banking and finance friends who set up huge accounts in Kabuki Bank so he can buy distressed office properties and expand Little Osaka toward the Ferry Building. Bill competes by expanding Chinatown through our sleepy SOMA, all the way to AT&T ballpark. Mayor Tiffany's bank and Kabuki Bank play Monopoly for real. They compete to buy up downtown so it does not become only Chinese.

As much as the City needs the money, the feds are obviously worried because of the growing military tensions in the China Sea and fears of secret codes in consumer products and financial systems. The City sits at the tectonic plate between China and the U.S. and at ground zero of the new AI boom so everything is going crazy. Our Little Osaka has triggered a new Pacific trade war. I'm just a high school kid who does not know much about Asian politics, except for a few lessons we get in class. I'm as clueless as most Americans about China, Japan, Korea, India and the rest of Asia. We buy their products and eat their food but only get a sampling of their politics in school.

We cross our fingers. Maybe Bill's C-Pop City, a "soft power" approach to downtown to avoid scaring critics of China, will work. After all, the City focuses on consumer products and entertainment, not military electronics like Silicon Valley. We just want to fill our offices, play games and have fun with friends.

How do we balance national rivalries? As a former "Top Gun" trainer in high-stakes conflict, Mayor Tiffany mentions the strategy book that she's preparing.

To our relief, Bill and Mayor Tiff get along dandy. He offers to invite his Chinese American and Chinese corporate buddies to invest heavily in downtown. Chinatown folks cheer since downtown has encroached on Chinatown since the 1870s. For the first time in century, Chinatown is encroaching onto the financial district.

It's historic, but the media and bloggers post Hearst-like "Yellow Fever" headlines: "China Invasion!", "Gold Mountain West!", and "Dim Sum Economics." Midwest papers talk about Chinese corporations buying up farmland. The East Coast media raise horror stories about Chinese spies and femme fatales, a sure way to attract eyeballs and ad revenues during their slow news periods. Unfortunately, it works so Mayor Tiffany is bombarded with journalists looking for "Chinese spies" as though the City is ridden with Chinese horror stories. Hollywood is even worse. It sends teams into downtown to dig up allegations and innuendos to write lurid and frightening spy thrillers. Soon, streamers run China Noir series about Chinese spies and gangs in SF, LA, Seattle, New York City and other cities where Chinese live, making every Chinese American a suspect since most Americans can't tell the difference between Asian Americans. It's a nightmare come true: a new "Yellow Fever" hysteria over imagined Chinese spies everywhere, with the media and ideologues making fortunes.

Poor Bill gets the brunt of the media accusations. He's tied to Chinese investors and corporate money, thanks to his very large family, so the media investigates each member as though they were gang members or spies. Given the growing anti-China hysteria, Bill says his family is careful to follow all laws and guidelines, but it doesn't work. They still get investigated, just like we Japanese Americans were after Pearl Harbor. History repeats itself.

Mayor Tiffany asks Steve Durbin and me for help. Steve is half Japanese and lives near my family in Japantown so has double credibility coming from the Black and Japanese communities. Mayor Tiff wants us to defend our Chinese bros from unfair media and political attacks. We are asked to stand up for AAPI rights. I'm being thrown into anti-Chinese lion's den and way over my head, but this is way more important than printing robots and my tiny Maker village plans. Our entire team is now in the global spotlight. How can we help Bill promote C-Pop without the media sensationalism and political attacks? The City is already the darling of urban critics so we do not need more trouble. Our downtown is dying so we need answers and action fast.

Bill doesn't waste time. With our Little Osaka team, he creates a pan-Asian alliance to support Chinese Americans so we don't end up with more anti-Asian hate crimes and attacks. Mayor Tiffany, Steven, Yamaguma-san and I lead the charge. I never expected to get into racial politics, but SF is the Asian American capital so we cannot ignore American politics and geopolitics. It's all connected.

18

TATTOO CITY

When I'm down and out
With my tattoo finery
I look for angels

The anti-Chinese hysteria is so bad that Mari and I want to do
something positive. We brainstorm and decide on a Tattoo City
initiative with veterans so we can wave the American flag. It works.
Many of Mari's Goth friends are vets. Most fought in Iraq and some
in Afghanistan so they are a tough bunch. They protect Bill from
political attacks. My tattoo friends and Mari's veterans proudly wear
our tattoo legs. Bill invites Asian American vets. Mayor Tiffany
wants a show of force. She invites the armed forces – the Air Force,
Army and Marine vets – and the Coast Guard and National Guard.
Market Street looks like V-Day with thousands of veterans and their
families cheering our tattoo leg parade and giving hugs to veterans.
Bill's Chinese vets and I ride a Tattoo Vets float and we dress in
military fatigues. I wear a cosplay version.

My father is so proud of me that he establishes a Tattoo City
studio as part of Little Osaka. Mari, Yumi and I invite paraplegics
who want to get cool tattoo legs printed by Brad's team. Within
weeks, people seeking tattoo legs pour into town so Mayor Tiffany
hosts a Tattoo City Day to get sponsors to provide free legs. Soon
we are a huge tattoo community. I didn't realize there were so many
people with artificial legs. People get rid of their ugly stumps and
replace them with tattoo legs of all colors, sizes and shapes. My
father sponsors a Tattoo Leg contest so the top designers can show

their tattoos in our first-ever Tattoo SF fashion show. I'm so happy that everyone pitches in. That's one thing I like about the City. When we have problems, we don't just argue, but dream up new ways to do things better. The artists and Makers are usually the first ones to invent new ideas, then the techies and our communities, finally politicians. But at least everyone jumps in after a while.

Our Tattoo City parade, exhibits and fashion shows attract the media and people from all over the world. My father finds sponsors for a Tattoo Expo at Moscone Center. We get dozens of engineering, design, and materials companies to host us. Before we know it, we host the biggest Tattoo Expo in the world for legs and other body parts. My favorites are arms and hands, which are soft and realistic. You can't even tell they are artificial, except for the see-through tattoos.

My father is so proud. Mother and her friends used to laugh at his dreams about Akihabara West. Now they support us. After I lost my leg, my mom doubted I would succeed. Now our Tattoo City is attracting Osaka robot makers and tattoo designers. She invites her friends to show off Little Osaka. Japanese travel agencies are organizing Little Osaka tours, which attract local government officials trying to revive their dying towns and attract young people and artists. My father and I are interviewed by the Japanese media, which wants to know how our "San Francisco magic" can be transferred to Japan.

My father has it memorized from repeating it so often: "If you want lively artists and young people, invite gamers, tattoo designers, e-bikers and cosplayers, then your sleeping towns will wake up. How about creating cool San Francisco East districts? If we can create Little Osaka here, the sky is the limit in Japan. We can help you."

My dad is a genius. His words inspire dozens of Japanese cities to create San Francisco Cool districts in their struggling downtowns and Brad, Mari, Yumi, and my friends and I are asked to supply our artwork and products and offered free flights to Japan. Some towns even print little Golden Gate bridges and specialize in 3D printed products for elders. They love tattoos of local fairytale characters. How cool is that!

19

ROBOTVILLE

Robots are coming!
Watch your backs, my fellow bros
They are friends, not foes

Ayako's Tattoo City is amazing but I have to get my butt into action. I've been spending so much time helping her with 3D tattoo printing and exoskeletons that I've forgotten my own passion: robots! I want a Robotville in Akihabara West that can show every possible type of robot: ant bots, dog bots, humanoids, construction bots, surgery bots, transformers, sex bots, and mentor bots. If I can do that, I would be in paradise and wouldn't get stuck in mother's Kimono Minds shop all day. I could invite robot inventors from all over the world and turn SOMA into the "Robot Kingdom" that I've dreamt about since I saw Star Wars and Astro Boy. My friends wanted to dress up like Darth Vader and the Jedis, but I wanted to look like 3C-PO, so I wore robot clothes since first grade. My sisters think I'm crazy, but they're no different. They dress up in Goth, cosplay and virtual fashions. It's different costumes for different folks. My bots are just cooler and harder to design.

How can I build Robotville? I ask Yamaguma-san if he can set aside several offices and storefronts for my robot friends. After hesitating, he says OK. His offices are half empty so he has nothing to lose.

"Do you need any help from Japan?" he asks.

"Help?" I reply. "I need everything. Robot designers, makers, electronics, materials, everything! Can you get them?"

"Not easy since I'm a banker, but I'll ask."

Yamaguma-san goes into action like a kid, asking every robot company in Tokyo and Osaka if they would open shop in our little Robotville. To our surprise, dozens send reps to investigate our empty offices. They want to expand into the U.S. Yamaguma-san signs contracts with some companies and boxes of robots and parts start arriving at our offices. I am over the moon. Our Makers welcome them with sake parties. We smack a huge sake barrel open with wooden mallets to celebrate our opening, attracting thousands of Makers, Star Wars fans, and bot designers who pour into our offices inspecting everything. Many enter short leases to set up shop in our new co-working/co-living spaces. Our Robotville is coming life like my Pinocchio robot!

I am so happy that I can't sleep at night or focus on school work. Robotville is my new school. In fact, for many of us Makers bored in class, it is our school so Yamaguma-san talks with local community colleges and robot makers to establish a robot school where people can learn all about them and create their own bots. Within a month, thousands sign up for online and in-person classes. Robotville soon looks like a mini-factory, with Makers creating bots and smart e-bikes as part of their class assignments. We have show-and-tell sessions, demos, stress tests, contests, fundraising shows, exhibits and even a conference. The City has become the "Robot Capital." Steve Durbin flashes a copy of Tokyo University Professor Mori's famous book, "The Buddha in the Robot," and merges his Soul City with Robotville. His bros build dancing bots that boogie to rap, hip-hop and reggae songs. Robotville is rocking with dancing bots that make the rest of Akihabara West look sleepy.

"We have arrived!" yells Steve over the loud music. "Our dancing bots have landed. Take that, NASA! Your Mars bots are nothing compared to ours."

Within months, Yamaguma-san and his robot sponsors have created the fantasy playground that he and I always wanted. At heart, we're both kids who never grew up, like Disney, Lucas and Spielberg. If we can have fun doing business like this, why would anyone want to grow up and become boring like everyone else? The City is for Dreamers like us.

20

GREEN FASHIONOPOLIS

When the hemp turns green
Filling our permaculture
Our fashions blossom

Akihabara West has triggered so many initiatives that we cannot keep up: Cosplay City, Little Osaka, Soul City, C-Pop City, Tattoo City and now Robotville. My father, Brad and I are happy but Emi and their mother look unhappy and say something is missing. Curious, I sit down with them to find out why.

"All the fancy cosplay, robots, tattoos and soul music are great," says Emi. "My cosplay outfits are selling well, but they are just more fast fashion. We don't need to pollute the Earth with more throwaway stuff. I agree with Mayor Tiffany that the City needs to go green and promote a regenerative fashion industry."

"What's that?" I ask, not knowing a thing about the latest fashion buzzwords.

"Everything recycled – textiles, plastics, old clothes, jewelry, hats, shoes, and bags – and designed with new biomaterials."

"Biomaterials?"

"From hemp, cactus, pineapple leaves, grape skins and seeds, banana stalks, algae, orange peels and other plants. I read you can make vegan bio-leather from mycelium, the threadlike part of fungi."

"That sounds like cooking class. Can you eat it?"

"No, but you can use it as compost. It's the latest trend in fashion so we need to own it."

"How do we do it?"

"We already have fashion schools, art schools, naturalists and green designers in the City. We need to invite them to Cosplay City and ask them to show their latest fashions."

"Have you talked with Mayor Tiffany about your idea?"

"Not yet. That's why I'm asking you and your father to help since Akihabara West and Little Osaka are so successful. Mayor Tiffany will listen if we talk business."

"Let's do it. I'll ask my father to invite her to Kabuki Bank."

Mayor Tiffany is so excited about our – or rather her – idea that she hurries to meet us. Brad's mother joins us. My father pours green tea and we sit around his conference table, which is lined with kimonos made from biomaterials in Japan. Mayor Tiffany is impressed.

"How do they create those gorgeous kimonos?" she asks, wide-eyed like a child. "I've never seen regenerative kimonos before."

"They're new in Japan," says Mrs. Morioka. "It's the latest rage in Kyoto among young designers. These photos are from their latest green fashion show."

"Green fashion show? That's what we need to do!"

"What's stopping you?" asks my father.

"Money woes, supervisor opposition to new programs, red tape, the usual..."

"I can organize a green fashion show in Little Osaka so you don't have to ask for City money or approval. We'll hold it in empty offices. I'll set up space for pop-up shops or co-working spaces."

"That's exactly what we need to revive downtown! How soon can we start?"

"Today," says Mrs. Morioka. "My friends are waiting. They can come if you invite them."

"No problem. The City would be happy to welcome them. We'll ask the Osaka-San Francisco Sister City leaders to host Osaka. It's about time they reconnect with us."

"Kabuki Bank can also invite our Tokyo friends," says my father. "We'll show them how to do green fashion."

"Then it will be a full-scale green fashion battle between two cities," says Mayor Tiffany. I love it! That ought up wake up our supervisors who always nix my ideas."

"That's why Japan is our best friend," says Mrs. Morioka. "Without it, we would have to invent friendly robots and regenerative fashion using biomaterials. We need fashion designers, not just scientists. I don't think their designs would be very appealing."

My parents smile; they have not looked so happy in a long time. Before, they were always arguing about staying in San Francisco. Now they argue about which Japanese group to invite. Now I don't have to worry about my mother returning alone to Osaka. We can stay together as a family. Mayor Tiffany senses that so she does everything in her powers to keep us together – our family and our Osaka ties. That's why we love her so much. She is the coolest mayor we have ever met. I wish all mayors were open, friendly, smart, cool and stylish like her. Maybe if we had more women mayors, cities would not have so many problems.

My father, Mrs. Morioka and Mayor Tiffany move fast. They invite their friends from Osaka, Tokyo and other major cities to help us launch a Green Fashionopolis – Mayor Tiffany's latest concept. She wants to turn the City into the leading regenerative fashion center. Now she has the money and sponsors to do it: my father's bank and his Japanese business friends.

My father and mother laugh and chat over tea about green fashions and how they can invite their friends. I'm so happy for them. Secretly, I was afraid they would get divorced like many unhappy Japanese couples and move to different cities, but now they are back together. We are finally a family again. My mother fusses over my tattoo legs since she has ordered one for each day of the week for my birthday. I thought she hated tattoos since they are popular among the yakuza gangs in Japan, but Brad printed such beautiful tattoos that she is proud of them. I'm in paradise!

Our Green Fashionopolis comes alive quickly. My father sets up pop-up stands and runways in our larger offices so designers can easily set up shop to show their designs to shoppers and buyers. Our Fashionopolis becomes the hit of the fashion world. Every fashion company, photographer and retailer shows up for our pop-up green fashion shows so photos are everywhere online. My mother dresses in a beautiful lemon kimono made from hemp and tea leaves, designed by Mrs. Morioka's top designer friend. Mayor Tiffany wears her traditional green hemp gown, but adds new biomaterials to her shoulders and tail that look like waterfalls. The media goes wild. They love our shows and share their videos and photos everywhere. Without spending a dollar, San Francisco has become the Green

Fashionopolis, thanks to my father, mother and Mayor Tiffany. They are now fashion royalty in Japan and receive honorary citizen awards from Osaka, Kyoto and Tokyo. They shock me and the Japanese press by actually hugging before the cameras. Is my dad using a new type of incense in our offices?

21

EXOSKELETON KINGDOM

Prosthetic robots
Walking alongside humans
Algorithms trained

My Robotville is coming along nicely, but Ayako and Mayor Tiffany
have upped the ante with their Green Fashionopolis, which attracts
so much attention and free PR that I need to match them. My Maker
buddies say we're doing fine, but I can't let a Japanese newcomer
beat me. I'm from the City; we should own the place, not let newbies
show us up. Maybe I'm too much like my father who brought
Bunraku puppets from Osaka and competed with my mom's Kyoto
kimonos in a race to get free PR. No wonder my mother had me
manage logistics and advertising for her Kimono Minds shop; she
was competing for my attention and time. I was the grand master of
scrambling for both since we never had much money, especially after
my father died.

That's an idea: I'll dedicate Robotville to my father. He
always thought robots were more than toys and soldiers. They could
help people as 3D printed arms, legs and hands, walking aids,
construction machines, police patrols, blood vessel repairs and a
million other useful things. His Bunraku puppets were his way of
showing me how to invent new robots. In a way, Bunraku was an
early form of robots. He created puppets as language tutors, talking
parrots, dancers, monsters, ghosts and etiquette trainers. He had so
many ideas that our garage is filled with puppets and my robots. I
used many of his ideas in my robots. It was a way of honoring and

remembering him. My buddies and I would compete to build the coolest robots and enter them into local contests. Mine always had cool Bunraku styles. The biggest showdown was Stanford's Exoskeleton Contest sponsored with the Veterans Administration. We would see cool exoskeletons for all types of physical aides, ranging from transformer armchairs to para-gliders. I love these exoskeletons since they resemble my father's fancy Bunraku puppets.

How can I create an Exoskeleton Center to honor his animistic belief that all robots and puppets have souls like rocks, trees and people? My bible, of course, will be Professor Mori's "The Buddha in the Robot." I'll share with it everyone. Why not show the spirit of robots using exoskeletons? What kinds of demos and exhibits would get people to see robots and exoskeletons as more than just hunks of metal and plastic but actually filled with the spirit of their Makers, like my dad did?

Yoko Hamabe! She's a solar sculpture designer from Osaka who creates sculptures that move like robots. They are designed as beautiful dancers who move to the rhythms and music pouring from their loudspeakers. Her sculptures are huge, some over fifty feet high, with towering legs and long, slender arms with solar panels as fans.   She is a national treasure in Japan and the Bay Area. Burning Man fans love her moving light sculptures that sway to music and change colors to the mood. Thousands of people come to see her sculptures every night, which are programmed to dance with tunes. Like my father, she gives life to steel and plastic. Her sculptures are artistic exoskeletons that go far beyond my robots and 3D printed prosthetics. She is an artist; I'm Maker who can learn from her.   So I invite her to Robotville to get some ideas.

"Thanks for coming," I say. "We want to know how you would transform our robots into something totally new."

Yoko walks around our robots and exoskeletons and pauses a moment to mull over ideas. She holds a small talking robot designed like a rabbit.

"Very Disney-like. Do you like animals?"

"I have gophers at home."

"Do you talk to them?"

"All the time, especially when I'm stressed out."

"And you hold them?"

"Always. Why?"

"I always thought that robots were too mechanical and not lifelike enough. They need to have more life."

"Like Pinocchio."

"Exactly. Robots and puppets are great, but they are only as good as their puppeteers. No great storytelling, no interest."

"You sound like my dad. What do you recommend?"

"Focus on storytelling like he did, not just on cool designs and algorithms. You want living Pinocchios, not lifeless puppets."

"Like your dancing sculptures."

"I created them in the image of my mother after she died. She used to dance in the annual Obon and I always remembered her face, so happy and beautiful, when she danced in a circle on the podium, like a beautiful sculpture, but alive and smiling. So I design my sculptures in her memory."

"Wow, that's deep. I didn't realize that."

"Most people never ask, but think I only create beautiful things as an artist, not as a human with feelings. That is not art. That is artifice. Real art is filled with spirit. It is living, just like my mother, you, me, animals, and trees. We are all living art, but don't realize it."

I sit back, stunned. I never thought of robots, sculptures and exoskeletons as living, but only as physical versions of us. I saw them like buildings – solid, static and mechanical. I only worried about how they looked and functioned, not how they made us feel or even if they had a spirit. The first time I got an idea of Yoko's thinking was when Ayako put on my tattoo leg. She was no longer sad and hopeless, but suddenly came alive, as if Tinker Bell had waved a magic wand over her. For her, my tattoo leg had a life of its own; it gave her a new life. Maybe that is the magic of robots, sculptures and exoskeletons. They are projections of our spirits dancing, singing and walking about.

"Your father was a master Bunraku puppet maker, not because he created sophisticated traditional designs, but because he innovated. His puppets came to life like real people. His puppets became him, like Jim Henson."

Henson, my hero! As a child, I always watched The Muppets and wondered how he brought them to life. They seemed so real, like my friends, when they argued and roughhoused. The Muppets were my best friends, just like my robots and my father's Bunraku puppets. We all lived in a world of living puppets and robots, but did not think of them as spirits, just play and fun. My mother and sisters used to laugh at our childishness, but she and my sisters did the same thing with their kimonos, Goth outfits, cosplay and virtual avatars. They played make-believe and brought their fashions to life. We were all puppeteers and storytellers without realizing it.

"Focus on bringing your exoskeletons to life. Create things that matter to people, like Ayako's tattoo leg, then your exoskeleton kingdom will come to life."

"That's it! I'll call it my Exoskeleton Kingdom! Like Disney's Magic Kingdom, but way cooler and more hands-on."

"Make it yours. Copy the masters but transcend them. Make them truly San Franciscan. Make them real."

Excited by the prospects, my Maker friends and I hurry to create our little Exoskeleton Kingdom. We create exoskeletal dogs that bark and jump, birds that chirp, and trees that sway and talk. Soon, our little kingdom looks like a magic redwood forest of foxes, squirrels, hawks and skunks. Our robots, puppets, fashion and dolls merge into a playground of exoskeletons.

Ayako cheers us on. She likes the squirrels since they remind her of a forest near her home outside Osaka. The deer remind her of Nara Park. I showed how to use a game glove to control their exoskeletal heads and arms, an idea I got from my father's Bunraku puppets.

"Whee!" she says, laughing as she makes the squirrel swirl and dance like a ballet dancer.

I grab a skunk and make it dance with her squirrel. Ayako furrows her nose with distaste and her squirrel dashes away. My skunk chases it.

"Ugh, you smell!"

"Don't worry. I didn't add spray, but I could."

"Odor technology! I'd like to see that."

Like kids, we play with my exoskeleton bots and spend more and more time designing new ones, especially for her prosthetic friends who want to learn 3D printing for exoskeletons. Many want to print legs for their friends so they form an Exo-Excel Club for high-performance training. We are so popular that we attract Para-Olympic medalists and coaches who ask us to design new, state-of-the-art sports exoskeletons. We are hot!

Ayako and I spend so much time together that people think that she's my new girlfriend. Not really. Just a buddy, but she is cute, especially the way she laughs when I screw up. I never blushed before, but now I do regularly. I like her but I better focus on my exoskeletons. My girlfriend might get pissed off.

Getting back to business, I prepare an Exoskeleton Kingdom plan with advice from Yoko, my Maker buddies, Steve, Yamaguma-san and my sisters. I design a cool center in Akihabara West that looks like a Maker's dream fantasyland and workshop. My buddies are ecstatic and bring their friends to rent co-working space so we can work together on projects. Within weeks, we have dozens of Makers who bring their robots, exoskeletons, dolls, cars, cranes and other autonomous devices. We host the first Exoskeleton Show, which attracts thousands of kids and their families interested in robots and engineering careers. Yamaguma-san invites Japanese robot CEOs for a Japan Exoskeleton Show, where carmakers show their wearable exoskeletons that transform into e-mobility vehicles. The transformer robots are so trippy that the media pours into Little Osaka to get visuals of them shape-shifting from prosthetics into cars and robots and back again.

The coolest thing is that Cal, Stanford, MIT, Kyoto and Tokyo universities and robot companies contact me so they can set up workshops and send student interns to work with us. Thanks to Yamaguma-san's backing, we are the Exoskeleton Kingdom! I get an education from professors and their students by watching, listening and working with them. Cal and Stanford are recruiting me for the freshman class since I'm a junior. My robot dreams are coming true, but I have to get my grades up and ace the SATs.

"My father and I are so proud of you," says Ayako, giving me a big hug. "You printed my leg and saved his bank. Now we have a bright future together."

Ayako hugs me again, which is unusual for a Japanese girl, but I hug her anyway. Imagine that: my simple 3D printed tattoo leg led to Akihabara West, Tattoo City, Little Osaka, and now Exoskeleton Kingdom. It feels like a dream. I hope it isn't. I'll let my robots pinch me.

22

WOMEN POWER!

Bros rule the rosters
Filled with hubris and anger
Women rising up

Mayor Tiffany is different. She acts like a gamer bro, but wears green gowns. Powerful women in Japan act like men; they cannot show their femininity. Mayor Tiffany is both. She is a she-woman who orders men around city hall like servants. Steve says she learned that in the Mission protecting him and others from gangs. She became their peacemaker and settled gang fights with her brains and charm. But she can be soft like her mother who runs a cute shop in the Mission where people can buy clothes from Mexico. I want to be like her: strong but caring. My mother is strong but too much like my grandmother. My father calls her "a velvet glove over a steel fist." He listened to my mother or else no smiles and dinner. Women power!

Mayor Tiffany takes it to another level. She faces powerful men all day and night. The pressure must be huge. I cannot imagine how she survives political attacks from all sides. San Francisco is like a dogfight. People criticize her for everything. The media makes fun of her. Steve says: "In SF, the squeaky hinge gets the wheel." I find that a strange idea. Why not just grease the hinge before it squeaks? But this is America. People love to complain, argue and fight over everything. Male egos are big so women have to be strong like Japan, but tougher. You cannot look weak here. I guess it's a good lesson for me if I want to stay here. Better to be strong like a samurai.

What I like about San Francisco is the way powerful women

leaders like Mayor Tiffany rule. They act like the ancient empresses in Japan who ruled with kindness and strength. If you obeyed them, you're OK. If not, watch out. I'm surprised that Mayor Tiffany, congresswomen and women senators gather like men. In Japan, powerful women are few, but here they rule the nest. If you want to get anything done, Mayor Tiffany is the person. You either obey or you are pushed aside for someone who can deliver. She is like a soldier since she trained in the Navy. How fascinating: a woman fighter pilot! I grew up with a strong mother and sisters, but this is a strange new world of women rule for me. Someday, I want to be strong like Mayor Tiffany. That is my American Dream. I'm a Dreamer like all immigrants begging to get citizenship, but I'm lucky since my father is a banker with a strong wife. Without her, nothing would get done. Kabuki Bank would have failed years ago. Only my mother's support kept him afloat when he was failing and tenants were leaving. Without her, our bank would not exist. We would not be in the City. My father would not have created Akihabara West or Little Osaka. I would not have started Tattoo City. We would be stuck in Osaka. We cannot fail. We must be strong like Mayor Tiffany and my mother.

Mayor Tiffany takes the lead. Brad's mother and sisters and I work with her to build our Green Fashionopolis, which is led by women and girls. We rule shopping because men are shopping "zombies" totally out of touch with women shoppers. We organize green fashion shows and dance performances so all women and girls around the Bay Area can come to the City to design their green fashions and show them in fashion shows and dances. Within months, fashion magazines call us the "UN of Green Fashion" since we have hundreds of cultural and ethnic groups participating.

Our biggest surprise are the indigenous peoples who bring their thousands of tribes around the world to the City to show their Indigenous Fashions, which nobody has ever seen before. The tribes perform their sacred dances, which remind us of the annual Obon dance. Mrs. Morioka, my father and mother and I invite Japanese Obon dancers to join in. Soon, Korean, Taiwanese, Thai, Filipino, Malaysian and other indigenous tribes join us, then tribes from Africa and Latin America. Before long, we are the "UN of Green Fashion." As Mayor Tiffany likes to brag: women rule and dance!

23

KABUKI SHOWTIME!

Puppets and gamers
American Kabuki
Chaos all around

Yamaguma-san, Mayor Tiffany and I are cheering since we got our
wishes. We have attracted puppets, gamers and cosplayers, oh my! I
feel like Dorothy stepping into a colorful 3D world of dancing
villagers. Once dead, downtown is coming alive with Maker robots
like my father's Bunraku puppets, not all at once, but one block at a
time. Mari's Goth, Ayako's Tattoo City, Yumi's cosplayers, my
Robotville, Steve's Soul City, and Mayor Tiffany's Green Fashion
fans are renting offices in Akihabara West and Little Osaka. We have
become a Noah's Ark in the face of mass exodus emptying cities.
We are not the only ones. Seattle, LA, Chicago and New York City
are ghosts of their former selves, but we are the worst hit and sinking
faster than other cities, so their leaders and planners are coming to us
for advice. Do we cities have futures? What are they? Can we
duplicate Akihabara West or something similar? Can you help us?
Will it be enough? Who knows? There are no guarantees. My father
loves to quote Yoda: "There is do or not do. There is no try."
    Kabuki Bank is working hard. Yamaguma-san and I feel like
puppeteers trying to give life to our lifeless City. How would my
father have created the greatest Kabuki show on Earth using
Bunraku puppets? What stories would he have told? Ironically, as a
robot Maker, I'm the new puppeteer. I'm creating our future with
tattoos, AI and exoskeletons. Nobody has ever done it before in an
ailing downtown. I feel like the first generation Issei who arrived

74

poor and hungry in the City who had to scramble to survive in a land of strangers seeking gold like them.

I look back at the Forty Niners, the Chinese, the Issei, the Filipinos, the Mexicans and hundreds of other immigrants who escaped poverty and tyranny in search of a better life, but finding only slummy downtown buildings and no business. They struggled to survive with nothing but their drive, hard work and imagination. By comparison, we have it easy. We have tons of tech, rich investors and global markets. The City has recovered after multiple stock market collapses. We are just going through our latest bust. But what is our next recovery? Can Little Osaka reverse our downward slide? I keep recalling Paul Simon's song, "Slip Sliding Away." That is us in spades.

Yamaguma-san, Steve, my sisters, Maker buddies, and Mayor Tiffany sit in our Little Osaka storefront, gazing out at Market Street, which has only a few pedestrians after work. We sip green tea served by Yamaguma-san, mulling over our future.

"Congratulations to all of you, especially Kabuki Bank," says Mayor Tiffany. "We're attracting visitors, but not enough. Only Little Osaka is thriving. The rest of downtown is still empty and dying. What can we do?"

There is total silence for a long time as we mull over ideas. We have tried nearly everything, but still it is not enough to move the needle. We only attract niche groups. We need the mainstream public and international visitors. How can we attract them?

"How about Soul City?" says Steve. "What if we turn SOMA into the new Motown?"

"How would that work?" asks Mayor Tiffany.

"We invite in the big artists and record companies to host a Summer of Love 2.0."

"Can you get any sponsors interested?"

"If we do something different from LA and New York."

"Like what?"

"Like the Metaverse. We have all the tech giants, LucasFilms and Pixar. If we host a global rap-and-roll festival, people will come."

"Rap and roll?"

"Rappers and street poets sing to hip hop, rock, rap, J-Pop, K-Pop and Indian music."

"They can do it in any city."

"Not if we involve your green fashionistas and Kabuki."

"How would that work?"

"Like rap, jazz and our downtown, we just make it up on the fly. There's no score sheet. We just freestyle it."

"Yamaguma-san, what do you think?"

"It could work," he replies. "I can ask my Osaka robot makers."

"Why robot makers?"

"Traditional Kabuki is OK, but too familiar, even with rap and rock. We need something totally new – totally San Francisco."

"What do you mean by that?"

"City artists are not famous. They are tiny innovators. They make up stuff from scratch, like your recycled green fashions, but they remain small and weird. We need something big and fantastic like Hollywood."

"What do your friends and sponsors want to see?"

"Something surprising."

Yamaguma-san sits back, sipping his tea, then gazes at the Kabuki posters on the conference room walls. There is dead silence. We try to imagine downtown's future, but nothing original comes, just more of the same. We all sit quietly, doodling and scratching ideas onto our notepads. It is silent, like the streets outside. We are lost in our imaginations and dreams. All is empty. We are stuck.

Yamaguma-san suddenly jumps to his feet.

"I got it! An American Kabuki show! We can put on the great Kabuki show in history, even better than Japan!"

"Please explain," says Mayor Tiffany, puzzled like the rest of us.

"Imagine that we give all artists, Maker and performers the scripts from famous Kabuki plays and ask them to create designs and perform them around downtown every afternoon and evening."

"At Yerba Buena Park?"

"Not just there, but in the canyon streets between the empty offices. Artists can perform their Kabuki stories to music and we could project their images big onto the high rises."

"Like Times Square?"

"But bigger and better. We can invite performers to perform at three or four venues everyday from noon till 11pm."

"That will cause traffic jams."

"We should pick quiet areas and encourage people to ride BART."

"Better not do it when the Giants or Warriors are playing at home."

"We can promote their games with our events and vice versa."

"Who will sponsor it?"

"My Japanese, Asian and American corporate clients. They need something now to fill their offices."

"How would that work?"

"The offices would be creative studios and operations centers for our performances. They would be busy since we would have so many events everyday, both small and large."

We sit back, stunned by Yamaguma's vision and audacity. A year-round American Kabuki show! Who would have ever thought of that besides a failing Japanese banker whose daughter has lost her leg and wears my tattoo leg? Sometimes, life is like my father's Bunraku shows. You never know what you'll get. Meanwhile, we can laugh and have fun.

"Yamaguma-san," says Mayor Tiffany. "You're on. You bring the sponsors and I'll bring security and porta-potties."

"You've got a deal," says Yamaguma-san. "This will be the great Kabuki show ever seen."

"So it's Kabuki showtime!"

Yamaguma-san wastes no time rounding up sponsors who are ready to abandon all hope and sell their downtown properties. Within days, he gets commitments of a few million dollars, which is barely enough to cover the first American Kabuki street shows.

The news gets out fast. Within hours, thousands of Bay Area artists, rockers, rappers, dancers and actors sign up to get paid for performing. Kabuki Bank's website is so popular that Yamaguma-san creates a streaming channel called American Kabuki. He studies Gangnam Style's massive hit that attracted billions of viewers and hires top J-Pop and K-Pop animators and gamers to create a Kabuki fantasyland that makes Disneyland look tame. Steve helps him since Virtual Fillmore already attracts tens of millions of visitors per week.

Ayako, my sisters and Maker friends are so excited that they drop everything. Before we know it, downtown is one big, happy family creating all sorts of wild rap, hip-hop and jazz American Kabuki tales and myths. Their performances are not only projected onto high rises but also onto low-hanging clouds so Bay Area folks can see rappers, dragons and Goth warriors dancing above the City. Needless to say, everyone wants to party and heads downtown. It makes the our big Land's End rock festival look tiny.

Soon, BART and the freeways are packed with tourists and visitors coming in from everywhere. The congestion gets so bad that people stay overnight to avoid the rush. Hotels love us. Creators rent offices in Little Osaka and around downtown so they can qualify for sponsorships and crowdfunding. Kabuki Bank's streaming channel goes nuts. Over two billion people see our nightly performances and share it with others. Soon, artists in other cities copy us so their downtowns light up. Even NASA satellites can see dead downtowns lighting up one by one. Our American Kabuki Festival has gone viral. A smart entrepreneur, Yamaguma-san franchises American Kabuki and licenses it to other cities. They are fixated on SF. Not only is SF filling up with visitors, pop-up shops, fashion designers and media studios, we are seeing grandparents bringing their families into downtown, the first time in years.

Mayor Tiffany cleans up downtown and cracks down on shoplifting gangs. Kabuki Bank gives micro-loans to street vendors. Tax revenues are flowing into city coffers so SF can hire more police and sanitation teams. To shame shoplifters, Mayor Tiffany requires them to wear orange and clean up streets, which is projected onto high rises with their names and faces.

"Our laughingstocks," says Mayor Tiffany. "At least the Pilgrims did something right."

What amazes us is the creativity of local artists and residents who perform American Kabuki versions of Chikamatsu's famous "Battles of Coxinga," "Girl at Dojoji Temple," and "Treasury of 47 Retainers." They know nothing about Kabuki so they go online and study the "onnagata" (men acting as women), "aragoto" (exaggerated, wild styles), "roppo" (stylized exits), "kumadori" (make-up with magical looks), "wagoto" (ladies' men), and "gidayu-bushi" (voice, samisen and dance). City folks take to the storytelling like ducks to water since they love to dress up, sing, dance and play. Yamaguma-san is the master puppeteer; he has gotten us to study and perform Kabuki with a passion.

Our heads are dizzy from all the studying, excitement, performances, visitors and new media startups. We are so overwhelmed by it all that we need to rest often, just "sittin' by the docks of the bay" listening to Otis Redding. Like our Buddhist priests who bless our events, we sit in bliss.

24

FLOATING WORLD

Artists and jugglers
Floating in a sea of tea
Little Osaka!

My father, mother and I are absolutely delighted. Everything is
coming along fine with Kabuki Bank. Our offices are slowly filling
up. Artists are bringing their talent: African AI art designers, Osaka
animators, French virtual Tour de France gamers, Thai virtual cuisine
kitchens, and Mongolian meditation workshops. There are so many
cultures that Little Osaka looks more like San Francisco than Osaka.
That is our goal: to bring Osaka to the world and the world to SF. I
pinch myself to see if I'm really awake. It all seems so unreal, like the
floating world of Edo that I read about as a child – filled with
artisans, samurai, shopkeepers and society ladies – all dressed in
traditional kimonos, yukatas and mompe. Little Osaka has a Retro
Look since our newcomers are dressed to code: regenerative street
clothes from recycled textiles and used outfits. Downtown looks like
a street fashion show. Everyone wears torn Levis with their national
outfits. Women like the Harajuku look, with cute animal patches,
and e-bikers like Mari's Goth look of faux leather and high boots. My
Tattoo City friends wear all sorts of 3D printed legs with different
types of tattoos: animals, monsters, zombies, French dames, Spanish
toreadors, motorcycles, and wizards. We are the "UN of Tattoos"!
Brad and his Maker buddies are wonderful; they print everything we

can imagine.

But there is just one problem: Brad's Kenyan girlfriend. She is worried that I'm falling for him and I am, but my friends advise me to keep my distance, so I try but it's difficult. Brad and I work so closely with my tattoo leg friends that we spend nearly half of our time together. I pretend it is just work, but my friends can see through my smiles. Yoko has hawk eyes.

"You can't fake love," she says. "It's written all over your face."

"I'm not in love with him."

"Then why do you spend so much time together?"

"To build Tattoo City."

"Every night till late and on weekends?"

"We're preparing for the big Tattoo Expo coming up in a month."

"So love of tattoos. I would be careful. Love has a way of sneaking up on you."

Yoko peers into my face; I blush and brush my hair over my face, but she laughs.

"So transparent. You're in love."

"No, we're just friends."

"The mind says one thing, your heart and face another. You can't fool me. I study emotions for my inspiration. Focus on your tattoos so you can think straight, even though your heart is telling you something totally different."

To celebrate our first annual Tattoo Expo, Yoko designs a beautiful solar sculpture of an e-biker with a see-through tattoo leg like mine, but it is unique. It transforms from a tiger tattoo into a moving tiger sculpture in her virtual model!

"Are you going to build it?"

"A surprise gift to SF and Tattoo City."

"Arigatou gozaimasu! I cannot thank you enough."

"You can. Just plan the coolest Tattoo Expo with Brad, but don't fall too deeply in love. That might cause problems for your future."

"Problems? What problems?"

"Love has a way of messing up projects. I know. I've had many close calls."

"Many?"

"Dozens. Did you know Japanese women artists attract guys are willing to help? So focus on your art, not the Makers."

Yoko leaves our Tattoo City co-working space, smiling like a wizard. No wonder she is professionally successful as an artist.

So the floating world of San Francisco is real, like the Edo block prints on my father's office walls. Guys are constantly floating in and out of my workshop. Akihabara West and Little Osaka are thriving. My Tattoo City is alive. Mari's Goth e-bikers are celebrating. Mayor Tiffany's Green Fashionopolis is off to a booming start. Emiko has her Cosplay City in Kabuki Bank's co-working space. Brad's Exoskeleton Expo is going big. We are all floating in paradise! My dreams are becoming reality. I just have to watch out for all the helpful guys...

PURGATORY

25

BARBARY COAST

Drifters and grifters
Floating into the City
Pigeon shit again!

All good things must come to an end and does it come quickly in the City. Our latest Gold Rush attracts a flood of lookers, seekers, lonely-hearts and the homeless, not just artists, sponsors, and visitors, who attract thieves, gangs, scams and grifters. The City is reverting to its Barbary Coast self. Downtown has become a circus attracting the poor who hear about our free food, housing, and entertainment and pour into downtown like a great tsunami. Red states join in by giving their homeless one-way bus tickets to San Francisco so they can "enjoy the California weather." In a perverse way, it makes sense since they would die in the freezing winters and boiling hot summers, harming their homespun image. Meanwhile, our open-arms "come and get it" welcome wagon is so successful that it lures the homeless seeking their California Dream by the hordes. We have become the "UN of Homelessness."

Newcomers overwhelm our new homeless shelters so they end up living on the streets near city hall. The media ridicules the City as usual, especially when their news is slow, even though we're accepting the poor and homeless from all cities and states like Saint Francis. We're the punching bag for bored journalists. Our good intentions are nice, but as my father always said: "The best-laid plans often go astray."

How do we deal with this relentless tide of homeless families, grifters, gangs and thieves? Yamaguma-san is not surprised; he said Osaka and Tokyo attracted all types of rootless people during the Edo period. Poor farmers and ex-samurai crowded into castle towns in search of work, food and shelter. They became the "floating world" that supported the shopkeepers, artisans, bars, red light districts and geisha houses. Unlike Noh, which served the nobility, Kabuki theater attracted everyone, including samurai, scroundrels and prostitutes. Fights became so pervasive that samurai swords were confiscated. Women were banned so men played the role of women, a bit like SF today. Our Barbary Coast is an American version of Kabuki, but we cannot totally ban guns.

How can we find our Way, as Buddhist priests advise my family? What can we learn from the past? How can we "build the future on the past," as my mother does with her Kimono Minds shop? Are we stuck in an endless cycle unique to the City or are we destined for greatness again? It's hard to say. Mayor Tiffany says we are not alone. Climate, political and war refugees are inundating cities around the world; we are just the most visible.

Yamaguma-san calls Mayor Tiffany after a series of robberies hits Akihabara West and Little Osaka. Organized gangs swarm into the City like the unattached "ronin" samurai, attacking shops and threatening visitors. Downtown has become a shit show again, like the "Dirty Harry" 1970s, just when our best-laid plans are taking off. What can we do?

"We're hiring more police and deputized citizens to protect shops and public places," says Mayor Tiffany. "We'll do everything possible to stop crime."

"But the federal government prevents us from clearing them from the streets," says Yamaguma-san. "The progressives want to rehabilitate them."

"We'll do both. I served in the Navy. We know how to instill discipline and order."

"Law and order."

"Not repressive, but not a zoo either. My job is to maintain public safety, sanitation and sanity."

Mayor Tiffany is facing the worst disaster in her career so

rivals are talking about ousting her. Elections are next year so she has to move fast. Unless we refill the empty offices downtown, the City's budget deficit will reach a billion dollars in a few years, which would lead to layoffs of police, fire, teachers, street cleaners and all the people we need to stay safe and open. We're in a race for time. We can't screw up, but need to hunker down and go all out!

Yamaguma-san looks outside at the homeless gathered outside Little Osaka pop-up shops. Shopkeepers are donating money and food, but it only attracts more homeless people, so they stop. Mayor Tiffany offers free food and expands community kitchens near city hall that recycle food from restaurants and supermarkets. It works, but it creates bigger squatter settlements downtown, not just in the Tenderloin. It's like feeding seagulls at Fishermen's Wharf; if you offer food, birds show up and fight over it. LA and Seattle surpass us in homelessness, but ours is concentrated along Market Street so the same blocks are repeatedly shown in the news. The gangs know better; they avoid the Tenderloin and focus on ritzy shops and chain stores around town so Mayor Tiffany assigns more police to the retail zones. As Steve says, the City looks like the streets of Baghdad so we have revived "Baghdad by the Bay."

The Japanese media beams images of Little Osaka in Japan. Yamaguma-san is famous. His gentle face, distinguished grey hair and business suit made of recycled textiles – yes, Mayor Tiffany's green fashion trend has reached him too – stand out in a sea of homeless people and J-Pop, Goth, cosplay and Maker fans.

"Kabuki Bank is proud to stand tall in San Francisco," he says slowly and gravely, standing next to Mayor Tiffany. "We believe in the City and its prospects for the future."

"What are you going to do about gangs stealing from Little Osaka shops?"

"We are working closely with the police and have organized volunteer citizen patrols by our fans."

"Who are they?"

"Our Makers, Goth, cosplay and anime fans are designing "Save SF" badges and logos for all citizen volunteers who help patrol Little Osaka."

"Only Little Osaka?"

"All of downtown," says Mayor Tiffany. "Little Osaka is providing a model for downtown districts so they can self-organize their community watch teams."

"How are they doing that?"

"Artists are designing their local badges, logos and outfits and learning self-defense from Japanese martial artists and the police department."

"Martial arts? Like kung fu and karate?"

"Also judo, which is easier for women and older people."

"So SF is turning into a Kung-fu City?"

"Not like Bruce Lee exactly, but we are prepared.

The media swarms over the judo, karate and kung fu trainers who Mayor Tiffany introduces to the media. Half are women; half are retired police and veterans. All are fit and alert. Cameras flash at the sight of fifty trainers dressed in their local downtown uniforms. The media blares headlines: "Karate City!", "Kung Fu Mayor!" and "The UN of Bruce Lee!"

"All of the uniforms are green and made from recycled materials and clothes by our downtown communities, K-12 students and even the homeless. In San Francisco, we don't believe in wasting anything – people, clothes, food and trash. We recycle everything. We are a Cyclical City."

Oh my god, Mayor Tiffany knows how to spin even the worst news into something new, innovative and exciting. No wonder she became a Navy "Top Gun" trainer. She eats problems for breakfast, lunch and dinner. Go, Navy!

The media loves the sight of martial artists and Mayor Tiffany dressed in regenerative uniforms with cool street fashion designs. They descend onto downtown to watch our officers and citizen patrols practicing their kicks and throws. Kids are fascinated, so karate and judo gi sales skyrocket downtown and martial arts schools pop up faster than grass dispensaries. Kids want to become Bruce Lee, their hero, so Bruce Lee tee shirts fill downtown.

"We are "Uniquely SF" as Mayor Tiffany proudly proclaims. "We may be down, but our police and citizens kick ass."

She is so proud of our community watch teams that they become honorary citizens who are invited to all City events and given free tickets to the Warriors, Giants and Forty-Niner games. As a result, the City has to turn away the flood of volunteers who apply for free martial arts training and the honor of wearing City uniforms and badges.

To honor our heroes, Mayor Tiffany erects a huge statue of Bruce Lee at Civic Center Plaza, with his iconic saying: "Be like water." It works. Instead of fighting and attacking each other, street people become kinder and helpful to each other. They flow like water during the free tai chi sessions offered by the City. Mayor Tiffany flows with the best of them.

26

NINJA!

Marauders strike hard
Villagers at their mercy
Ninja patrol teams!

Mayor Tiffany is trying her best to reduce crime downtown but our success in Little Osaka attracts more and more thieves who target shoppers and our stores. It becomes so bad that people stay away from downtown. My father is desperate for a solution and asks Steve for help. Steve served in Special Forces overseas so he knows how to deal with chaos. My father invites him to Kabuki Bank for ideas.

"We're not going to get rid of thieves the traditional way," says Steve. "They're too smart and organized for the police. It's a cat-and-mouse game for them. While the cats are away, they like to play."

"What can we do?" asks my father.

"The old-fashioned Japanese way: ninja."

"Ninja? What do you mean by that?"

"In the Army, we had night teams called "ninjas" who patrolled high-risk zones to protect against surprise attacks."

"Did it work?"

"Like a charm. We camouflaged our teams in street clothes so they didn't stand out like our patrols. The locals could not tell the difference since many of our teams were local residents who we trained."

"So you can do it here?"

"Mayor Tiffany and I have begun. We've recruited several hundred former homeless veterans from veteran groups who need jobs and are training them now in a secret location."

"Will they be ready soon?"

"Next week. Many of our vets are seasoned fighters so they don't require much training since they worked in urban combat. They just have to learn how to meld into the street without attracting attention."

"So ninja training."

"Exactly. We always admired how Japanese ninja could disappear into the night, scale walls, run lightly over rooftops, slip into windows, eliminate foes silently, and control their territory with only a few ninjas."

"Will the mayor announce it soon?"

"No news. They will operate in total secrecy. You and Ayako are the only people who know beside the mayor. Don't say a word. This is a battle for downtown."

"Thank you so much. I never thought I would ever see ninja today, just in the movies."

"Downtown is now a big stage. We are the training center for a national ninja program to defend downtowns from organized crime. It's secret so thieves don't know who, where and when we will strike. Remember: Loose lips sink ships."

Steve puts his finger to his lips. My father and I bow deeply in thanks. We will never say a word to anyone.

After Steve leaves, my father closes the door and offers a cup of tea while we chat.

"Ayako-chan, your accident has really changed our lives and the City for the better. I am so proud the way you and Brad solved your problem and opened my eyes."

"I had no choice. I don't want to return to Japan, at least now. There's too much to learn and do."

My father sips tea and pauses.

"Let me ask you a question: Do you love Brad?"

I almost drop my cup.

"Why do you ask?"

"You spend so much time together."

"We're busy organizing my Tattoo City."

"I know but he's spending more time with tattoos than robots."

"We can help more people, not just build robots."

89

"I know, but still…I wonder."

"If I fall in love with him, I'll let you know."

I sip my tea, ready to choke. He just smiles. My father is wise. As a banker, he reads character fast and sees through masks into the people's heart, like Yoko. They have X-ray vision. That's why my mother loves him. He reads her heart without her having to say a thing. He reminds me of my favorite movie, "Love Story," where Jenny says: "Love is never having to say I'm sorry." My father never has to apologize to my mother or me for ignoring our feelings. He is like a wise samurai. He always anticipates things. He makes life easier to deal with. The City will need his wisdom in the coming years. I'm so glad he is my father. I'm so happy we're staying.

26

SWAT WEST

Flies land on the food
Crawling about our City
Suddenly swatted!

Little Osaka was a zoo a few weeks ago, but has suddenly become quiet. The street gangs and thieves have decided to go elsewhere. What's going on? They know something I don't, but what is it? Are the police cracking down? I don't see anything different or unusual. No extra patrols or militarized teams. All I know is that Little Osaka is safe again, as though somebody has waved a wand over everything. I shouldn't complain. At least my Maker buddies and women don't have to worry about thieves stealing our robots and fashions. We can host open studios and labs again.

But something is definitely going on. At night, I see more homeless guys sitting around swapping stories. Why would they hang out in alleys where they can be attacked? Why not near city hall where they can get food, security and shelter? It doesn't feel right so I'll run a little test. I'll leave my Maker shop unattended for an hour to see what happens.

I sit in a friend's van nearby and we turn off the interior lights and wait. At first nothing happens then we see a few homeless folks amble by. They look inside. One grabs some power bars I left on the counter. The other looks around the shop, but touches nothing. They are not thieves, just hungry and curious, probably sensing a set-up, so they leave.

We wait five minutes but nothing happens. Then a truck pulls up and five guys with black masks pulled over their faces get out of the truck and enter my shop. One guy stands alert near the door while the others stuff their bags. Their operation is fast and efficient. They return to their truck and toss their bags into the back.

Suddenly, three figures emerge from the dark like ninjas and descend onto the truck. One thief pulls a gun but they shoot him with stun guns. The thieves scramble but the figures tackle and handcuff them. They are silent and fast. They brandish guns, batons and nets. They are not regular cops, but a SWAT team.

My buddy and I are stunned by Mayor Tiffany's strategy: a ninja-like SWAT team. No wonder Little Osaka is silent. The gangs spread the word fast.

I call Steve to confirm what I saw.

"Just routine security," he replies.

"No way," I say. "They look like ninja, not regular cops."

"You didn't see them."

"What?"

"I said you didn't see them. Capiche?"

"So that's Mayor Tiffany's strategy."

"Again, you didn't see anything."

I'm right. It's a SWAT team dressed up like ninja. Who gave Mayor Tiffany that idea? Was it Steve or is it common practice?

Night after night, my buddies and I park our car outside our empty shop and watch the SWAT teams sit silently in the alley. No gangs appear. The word is out on the street: avoid Little Osaka. The gangs move to other cities, which see a sharp jump in store break-ins at night. "Cops and Robbers" blare the news. "Can our cities stop the gangs?"

But like Little Osaka the thefts start declining in Oakland then other Bay Area cities. The media sends in hidden camera teams that report ninja-style SWAT teams emerging from the dark and busting the gangs. Mayor Tiffany's strategy works. All the cities are copying SF.

I invite Steve for coffee to learn more.

"You're right," he says. "Mayor Tiffany got the idea about ninja from Little Osaka."

"From who?"

"Yamaguma-san. He loves ninja movies so he thought it could work in Little Osaka. The City has tried, but nothing else worked so we gave it a try. As you can see, it's working better than we expected. The gangs are avoiding the City at night."

"What about during the day?"

"Plainclothes ninja dressed like joggers and yoga instructors."

"Too obvious."

"So we mix them up. Different fashions, different styles, different types of veterans."

"Veterans?"

"Yes, special forces retirees. At our ninja training camps."

"Where?"

"Top secret. Let's say they are all around the Bay Area."

I sit back, sipping my coffee. Amazing. Yamaguma-san got the idea from ninja movies. I knew he loves movies and games, but I never imagined he would suggest the idea to Mayor Tiffany. I go to his office.

"Why didn't you tell me about your ninja idea?" I ask.

"We didn't know if it would work," replies Yamaguma-san.

"But it works."

"At least for now."

"What do you mean?"

"Gangs learn fast so they'll find new methods. We need to be prepared. We have ninja, but we also need to think like the "Seven Samurai."

"How?"

"Combine our ninja with the police, citizens watch and the national guard."

"Is SF preparing for a big crime wave?"

"Perhaps. The Asian triads are organizing."

"Where?"

"I don't know, but we are being asked to keep our eyes open. If you see anything strange, let me know."

A chill runs down my back. Our ninja have stopped break-ins, but now Mayor Tiffany is preparing for bigger international gangs. Not more small potato gangs, but hardcore professionals with huge bank accounts. This is getting to become a scary cops-and-robbers game, but at least Mayor Tiffany and Steve have military connections and combat training. We may be in for one long crime war. Now all of their combat strategy gaming may finally come in handy.

28

CYBER WAR

Eastern avatars
Meet western cyber cowboys
Battling over gold

Mayor Tiffany expects gang thefts all over downtown so my father hires more ninja cops to protect Little Osaka, but we totally miss the big one: cyber attacks. Kabuki Bank is attacked by wave after wave of hackers. We need help from Steve and his cyber security buddies.

"Yamaguma-san," says Steve. "My team tested your site and you are highly vulnerable. You need to harden your systems."

"How much will it cost?"

"A hundred thousand, but cheaper than losing your customer accounts."

"Like Silicon Valley Bank?"

"Worse. All of your assets."

My father turns pale. He has never dealt with cyber gangs.

"How fast can your team move?"

"Tonight. They can provide a discount since you're so important to the City."

Steve jots down notes, thinking hard. He is an e-commerce genius and the first Black unicorn CEO so we trust him. He sits up.

"I got it. Tattoo avatars!"

"What?"

"Our cyber-security team can design tattoo avatars as bait."

"Bait?"

"They can pretend to be customer AI avatars who ask simple questions about their finances. It is just disguise. They will be your bank security avatars to stop the cyber gangs."

"I don't understand."

"Ayako, help me. Can you sketch tattoos that you would like to see the avatars wearing?"

"Anything to help my father."

"Make them attract and innocent-looking girls. Kawaii (cute) is best. We want every cyber gang to approach them."

I cannot believe Steve's idea: cute tattoo girls to attract crooks. That sounds like a manga story, but I'll do it to help my father. I sit down and sketch a dozen cute tattoo girls, which Steve gives to his cyber security team. Within hours, they create cute virtual AI avatars of manga characters with big eyes and cheeks wearing sexy clothes with tattoo patterns. My father uses them to welcome bank customers and it works. We get hundreds of new customers, mostly guys who love Japanese manga and anime. But within hours cyber crooks approach the avatars and try to break into their accounts. Steve's team blocks their entry, captures their identity and inserts bugs to track them. Soon, we see the cyber crooks as red dots on a global map. Most are from Asia, with a few from the Mideast, Russia and Africa.

"We got them!" says Steve. "Now we know exactly where they are, their identities and movements. I'll notify Interpol and all banks."

No wonder Steve is a unicorn CEO. He is so smart and fast that my father offers a reward, but he declines since he works for the City and cannot accept money or rewards. Instead, he suggests that my father donate to Black youth training programs in the Fillmore and Bay View, which my father is more than happy to do. So we stop crooks and help poor communities at the same time. That's why I love SF; it has so many cool people like Steve and his cyber security buddies who "pay forward," as he says.

EAST VERSUS WEST

Eastern triad lords
Gathering in cyber lairs
Big shootouts online!

Steve's teams are awesome. Their cute AI avatars stop the cyber
gangs from Asia cold, but the attackers never give up. Steve invites
Yamaguma-san, Ayako and me to his cyber security center in city hall
so we can see his team in action. Most are private coders hired for
projects. As we walk into the center, we see huge world maps
showing the cyber attack activity worldwide. The center looks like a
Pentagon war room in the movies. We sit at the conference table
surrounded by large screens. Red dots showing attackers as hotspots
blink actively.

"This is where most of the Kabuki Bank attacks are coming
from," says Steve, pointing to China and India. "They have the most
sophisticated gangs. We saw them in the Army. Now they are
coming for cities everywhere with different strategies: bank break-
ins, fake identities, ransomware and more.

"Can we protect against all of them?" asks Yamaguma-san,
with a worried look on his face.

"Not all, but we can slow them down until we can mobilize
more resources."

"From the City?"

"No, Homeland Security. They're covering our backs."

I whistle from surprise. I knew Mayor Tiffany and Steve
collaborated with the Pentagon and Homeland Security, but not to

the extent as this center.

"We're hiring retired veterans who want to help our cities. They're all over the world."

"In Japan too?"

"Some of my best teams are Japanese. They are zero defect guys so nothing gets past them. Like product companies, they are our quality assurance teams."

"Like cars."

"As we like to say in the military: If Japan didn't exist, we would have to invent it."

"And that's why Kabuki Bank is important."

"It's a cornerstone in our Japan-U.S. alliance. All of Japan and Asia are watching us, especially China. They face massive cyber attacks on their banks, businesses and government agencies so we are an urban lab. All of us are closely watching the Asian triads. They are tough and sophisticated. They compete with western gangs so it's an East-West game on a global scale."

"So that's why Mayor Tiffany and you are into war gaming."

"We call it simulations, not gaming which is for consumers. We're focused on protecting communities and companies from phishers and scam artists who are proliferating as we speak. It's not just about downtown revitalization and K-12 STEAM education. We have to stop cyber attacks. If you think downtown crimes are bad, you haven't seen anything. It's small potatoes compared to the trillions of dollars in e-commerce at risk globally."

"Trillions?"

"Tens of trillions. The City's losses are a rounding error compared to the huge losses potentially facing all cities in the future."

"You're gamifying everything?" asks Yamaguma-san.

"To make it fun for the public. Like military simulators, we run open contests to probe for weaknesses and break-ins. We're using AI quantum computers to stop the hackers."

"It's AI quantum race between China and the West," I say.

"Exactly. An East-West rivalry for AI and quantum supremacy to protect City assets, not launch cyber wars. That's why your sister Yumi is studying AI cybersecurity at Cal. It's our future."

"Wow, they never teach you that in high school. I never knew the Pentagon was involved."

"It's everywhere. You just don't realize it. And Japan is our closest ally in the Pacific so they're crucial to SF's future. Without Japan and Asia, our cities will not have a safe and secure future."

"Why does Kabuki Bank matter so much?" asks Yamaguma-san. "We are just a tiny bank."

"You are a target for cyber attacks. We need to learn how cyber gangs attack so we can defend the City from bigger attacks. They could shut us down overnight if we're not careful."

Yamaguma-san and I sit back and look at each other. I have read about cyber security, but never realized it was so critical to the City. I thought it was across the Pacific in the China Sea and Indian Ocean, not in our backyard.

"Brad," say Steve. "You're still young and learning about Asia Pacific geopolitics, which are confusing all of us. We are inventing the future and don't know what surprises it holds. Mayor Tiffany and I meet federal agencies regularly to discuss how to protect the City. I wish we had a crystal ball, but we don't. That's why the Pentagon appreciates Mayor Tiffany's and my military experience. We understand what's at stake. It's not just music, arts, education and business. It's about our national and local security. We sit on one of the biggest political fault lines in the world: East and West. What we do with Kabuki Bank and Little Osaka will determine the future of our City and the Bay Area."

I sit back and ponder. This civics lesson is scary. We are walking targets for every cyber scammer in the world. I'm glad our backs are covered.

"I am grateful for your help," says Yamaguma-san. "I will do my best to uphold our U.S.-Japan partnership."

"You're already doing a first-rate job," replies Steve. "Every branch of the U.S. government and our allies know all about you. We are all rooting for you. We want you and San Francisco to succeed. We are the Tech Capital so what happens here matters. It sends shock waves around the world. Maybe with you we will become the Culture Tech Capital."

Yamaguchi-san and I are humbled. We are tiny ants in a huge anthill, but we matter. Everything matters. My father would be proud of us.

29

BARBARY BAY

Cyber attacks galore
Fireworks lighting up the sky
Welcome to the bay!

Steve is not making up things. Before we end the meeting, a red alert begins. The screen fills with blinking red lights of cyber attackers descending onto San Francisco. It looks like a nightmare out of Dr. Strangelove, with cyber missiles coming in at an accelerating pace. At first, a few dozen then hundreds and finally thousands of attacks. The entire screen fills with blinking red lights.

My father is terrified. Steve grabs him to calm him down, but my father shakes as if having a stroke. Steve calls for a medic who rushes into the room and leads him to a sofa. I help him. My father lies down, shaking, so I get a wet towel and put it on his forehead.

"I'm OK," he says, trembling. "I just need rest."

"Get the blanket over there," says the medic. "Then hold his hand."

I rush to get a moist towel from the restroom and place it on my father's forehead. He looks pale. I'm worried about his health since he has been working overtime for months and looks weak. I pray he is strong enough for this challenge.

Steve takes my father's hand and strokes it gently.

"You're in good hands, Yamaguma-san," he says. "Everything will be alright."

My father looks up at Steve and me. There is fear in his eyes. I hold his hand tightly and he smiles.

"I am strong like you, Ayako-chan. We will get through this together."

I call my mother who rushes over and brings moist towels, water, a blanket, hot tea and some sweet mochi cakes. She places the extra blanket over him to be sure since he is trembling.

"Just stay here with him," says Steve. "The medic will bring anything you need."

"Thank you," says my mother. "You are so kind."

"It's my job. Your husband and family are very important to this City. Without you, our downtown cannot recover."

My father looks into my eyes then at my mother and Steve. He says nothing, but his eyes say it all: I love you all. Thank you so much. Since Steve and Mayor Tiffany encouraged him to open Akihabara West and Little Osaka, we have been reunited as a family. His vision has been the glue to keep us together and the City. My father always says: "Kansha (gratitude), we always must be grateful for the kind people in the City." I agree. When I lost my leg, I almost gave up my dreams. I wanted to die, but Brad, Steve and Mayor Tiffany rallied me on. They are my best friends. They cheered on my Tattoo City when others ignored my friends and made fun of us. It hurt, but our tattoo legs not only helped us stand up again, it helped us to stand up tall, proud of our legs. That is why I never want to leave the City. Our friends help you when you're down. No wonder the City was named after Saint Francis. People help you here, not attack or humiliate you like other places. I will never leave. My heart will always be here for the rest of my life.

The City goes crazy again with cyber attacks, but Mayor Tiffany, Steve and my father stand tall against them. They do not give up but help Little Osaka, Tattoo City, Makers, cosplay designers, gamers and musicians – all the little people. Our Little Osaka is a tiny village facing powerful cyber gangs like the village in "Seven Samurai." Steve and his veteran friends are our seven samurai. It's strange how life is like the movies.

Despite wave after wave of attacks, Steve's cyber security team stops them. He invites my father, Brad and me to watch the cyber battles on the big screen in city hall. It's like watching a video game, but it's real. We bring popcorn to watch the attacks and counterattacks like going to the movies. Brad and I cheer when Steve's team stops the attackers. He is our badass Toshiro Mifune! (Brad taught me that word). Brad and I watch our seven samurai in action again and again. We compare Steve's tactics with those of

Mifune and discuss how he copies Mifune and where he differs.

"I admit," says Steve. "I love Mifune. He is my hero. In fact, Mayor Tiffany and our Mission gamer buddies study "Seven Samurai" for inspiration and strategy. Mayor Tiffany applied his tactics when she was a "Top Gun" Navy pilot and team leader. I used them in the Green Zone. That is the only way we survived attacks in Baghdad."

"So this is Baghdad by the Bay," I say.

"You got it," replies Steve. "Just higher stakes since Japan, China and the rest of Asia are involved."

"How big?"

"Ten of trillions of dollars in investments, commerce, trade and infrastructure development."

"Everywhere?"

"Pretty much. We're just a tiny blip on the big geopolitical screen, but a strategically crucial one."

"How important?"

"Silicon Valley. Any more questions?"

"Does the Metaverse matter? I hear it's dead."

"Not for the military and enterprise. We use it all the time for war gaming."

"War gaming?"

"Running scenarios and simulating cyber attacks and real military battles."

"Like video games."

"Just bigger, more sophisticated and real."

"So that's why you, Mayor Tiffany and your veteran buddies stay close to the Pentagon."

"Let's put it this way. The Pentagon plays the biggest game in the world and the Bay Area is the tech capital for our Asia Pacific allies. Without them, the U.S. would be flying blind."

"That bad?"

"Totally at the mercy of military and cyber attacks. Defense is not just guns; it's data analytics. No data, no future. Our military, financial, utilities, government and commercial sectors would be shut down overnight."

"What about AI and quantum computing?"

"We're in a tech arms race and sit in the pilot's seat. That's why the Pentagon listens to Mayor Tiffany. She's the only American mayor who has flown in combat and graduated in data science so she has what we call "360 awareness." She knows danger and she's a "Top Gun" gamer to boot. You cannot find another mayor in the world with more military, computer, gaming and cyber-security savvy. She makes POTUS and most Pentagon boys look like amateurs in military simulation games."

Ayako, her father and I sit back, totally stunned by Steve's words. We knew the U.S.-Japan alliance was important but we did not know how big and important our City was to our Pacific shift and how crucial Mayor Tiffany was to the Pentagon. We always thought of cherry blossoms and chysanthemums, not swords.

"In Washington D.C., they call her the "Cyber Samurai". She is so smart and seasoned that nobody can match her geopolitical and war gaming experience and savvy. I'm just her sidekick."

Steve gets up and clicks to open a window on the big screen.

"Mayor Tiffany has asked me to develop an Urban Ransom game for the public. The AI game simulates a variety of cyber attacks for ransom. Players have to stop them using cyber security tools we provide."

"You're gamifying cyber security?"

"For our K-12 schools. Mayor Tiffany wants to train all City kids in cyber security, e-commerce and finance so they can get into colleges and useful tech jobs. It's part of her jobs program. No more low-paying gigs. They need high-paying jobs so they can stay in the City. We cannot afford to lose our young people. We need them to stay here since they know and love the City more than outside investors and developers. They're our future. That's why I've invited you and Ayako to see our tech operations. We want you to lead our young people."

"How?" asks Ayako, looking worried.

"By doing what you're doing, but integrating it into the K-12 curriculum. Mayor Tiffany is setting up tech hubs throughout the City, which are free to all K-12 students and their families. The hubs will provide high-speed Internet, desktops, tools, workshops and mentors. The City will host Grand Challenges, school rankings, awards, college credits and scholarships for high performers, funded by our corporate sponsors."

"We have them?"

"She's tapping her Stanford classmates and I'm working with

the Cal and CSU alumni for donations. This will be a Bay Area initiative, not just for SF. Mayor Tiffany wants all people, not just SF folks, to learn how to build with AI and protect their digital presence so they can get good-paying jobs."

"That's the mantra: good-paying jobs."

"Yes, that's the bottom line for cities and towns everywhere. No jobs, no future and no hope. We need to reverse the downward spiral of unemployment, drugs, despair, conflict, violence and crimes. Mayor Tiffany and I fought in Iraq so we know what hell looks like. We never want Baghdad by the Bay to look like the real Baghdad that we saw."

My father and I bow deeply to Steve. We are eternally grateful to his kindness and Mayor Tiffany's vision and leadership. We wish Japan had more mayors like her. Maybe it will someday.

"Oh, one more thing. Mayor Tiffany is inviting all Japanese and Asian mayors to visit the City so they can see our tech hubs in action. We will work with our sister cities around the world to share our knowledge, tech and sponsorships. Mayor Tiffany wants us to become the "UN of Green Tech" – without the greenwashing. She wants you to lead her Regenerative Fashion initiative."

"How?"

"She wants Tattoo City to create regenerative fashion for the rest of us – for all people, especially the weak, differently abled and aging. We all weaken as we age so we must develop exoskeletons and 3D printed prosthetics now for our aging societies. Japan is the fastest aging society so the City will lead with it. We're planning to invite groups of Japanese elders to co-develop our prosthetics. Ayako, you get to lead the teams."

"Me, the leader of regenerative fashion? I have never led anything."

"You will work with Brad who will be in charge of 3D printing, exoskeletons and biometrics."

"I would be more than honored," says Brad, saluting Steve.

"Cal and Stanford have asked me if you both want to be registered as early admit students because of your leadership with Tattoo City. They want to develop exoskeleton and regenerative fashion programs in their engineering and design departments. Mayor Tiffany and I know the professors and researchers who adore your work."

I am ready to cry. I cannot believe it. Cal and Stanford want us, two teenagers, to help them develop new programs? We are still high school juniors.

"Don't worry, Ayako. You don't have to know engineering. Your job will be usability design and testing. We want you and your Tattoo City friends to help engineers test their designs."

Steve pulls up a window on the big screen and shows virtual robots designed as seniors wearing exoskeletons and lifting barbells. An old lady boogies to music in her exoskeleton tights. The room is filled with baby boomers dancing to the 1960s Summer of Love rock music from their youth.

"If we're going to create exoskeletons for aging boomers, we might as well have fun and dance to golden oldies. It will open our Summer of Love 2.0 festival."

"With rock music?"

"And other global music by hundreds of Bay Area ethnic groups who will be invited to design exoskeletons for injured and aging people so they can dance to their own music. It will be a celebration of music, tech and the arts – a cultural Renaissance."

Steve pulls up a huge scene of people, young and old, dancing in different ethnic costumes and exoskeletons to rock music. It looks like Carnaval, except international and much bigger. The whole City is dancing!

I burst out crying since I never thought I would ever see paraplegic people dancing with tattoo legs. Steve's scene looks like something out of a fairy tale.

"Mayor Tiffany has come up with our slogan: San Francisco Rocks! Guess who is opening it? Santana! He'll get the party rolling. And we've invited LucasFilm and Pixar to provide dancing avatars of all ethnicities and types. We will have one gigantic City party and parades for an entire week to reopen downtown. Your father, mother, you, Brad and your teams will lead the parade with Mayor Tiffany and our team. You will be our Japanese tattoo princess."

I am stunned. Never in my dreams have I ever imagined that I would create a Tattoo City with Brad and lead a parade. I am in paradise!

31

VIRTUAL SMILES

When all is chaos
Just smile your troubles away
With your avatars!

Tattoo City is a wonderful spectacle with all the top tattoo and exoskeleton designers, prosthetic 3D printers, and regenerative fashionistas working smoothly together like the 49ers headed to the Super Bowl. Ayako and I are ecstatic; we are the new tattoo royalty! We are rocking and rolling with cool tattoo prosthetic designs – the first in the world -- so top designers, 3D printers and fashion designers are descending onto Tattoo City, filling Little Osaka with printers, pop-ups and tiny studios. Yamaguchi-san is delighted and places Maneki Neko cats in the lobbies, bars and restaurants to welcome newcomers and shoppers. Mayor Tiffany stokes the fires by wearing her eponymous green gowns and jewelry at press conferences, which attract hordes of journalists and bloggers. Ayako shows her latest tattoo prosthetic designs, which are copied around the world. She has become the new Prothetics Queen poster girl. Steve's coders build Tattoo City in VR so shoppers can walk around our virtual tattoo shops, pick designs they like and fit themselves with various prosthetic designs. It's like a high-end Paris haute couture shop, but totally dedicated to prosthetics. We're the first online 3D prosthetic printing business so we grab headlines, especially when Ayako wears cool Japanese happi coats and shorts to showcase her prosthetic tattoo leggings. She's a hit among girls who copy her.

     All is going well, but life has a way of intervening. Within weeks, hackers attack Tattoo City and deface our tattoo designs. Steve's cybersecurity team tries to stop them, but the hackers pop up again and again in a constant game of cops and robbers. For the next few weeks, Steve's teams and the hackers duke it out, with hundreds of hackers defacing Ayako's designs. We spend most of our time battling the latest hacks, but new ones pop up immediately.

"I give up!" says Ayako. "There's no end to hackers."

"We'll stop them," I reply.

"How? Steve is doing everything he can."

"He's working on a secret weapon."

"What is it?"

"I don't know. He says it's a surprise for your birthday."

"I hope it works."

Ayako polishes her leg so it shines for photographers who snap hundreds of shots. She is depressed but fakes her smiles like a pro.

"It hurts too much to smile. I'm not used to it."

"Welcome to California. Everyone fakes smiles for selfie shots and gatherings so get used to it."

"Can't we use fake AR smiles? We could design the perfect smile. Then people wouldn't get tired and have to fake it."

"Steve's team has them. His jazz musicians use fake smiles after his Virtual Fillmore jazz festivals."

"Why after?"

"To chill. It gets tiring to smile all the time."

"Like vaudeville?"

"Exactly, but even more so. They need to smile like airline stewards to keep customers coming. No smiles, no money."

"That must be tiring. I just want to be real."

"Don't we all."

Ayako slumps onto the couch after the shoot and I put a blanket on her so she can rest. She smiles like a princess. I caress her hair and grin. We are a great team. Just the two of us have changed the world of prosthetics. We could build Tattoo City into a major franchise together.

Ayako pulls me to her and smiles. I pull back but she pulls me closer. I'm nervous. I have a girlfriend or at least had one. She's busy with team sports so we haven't seen each other in weeks. Somehow, our lives are going in different directions, while Ayako and mine are converging like two rivers. I want to caress her beautiful, long black hair, which reminds me of the Heian princesses in

Japanese block prints. I have never caressed a girl's hair before so I'm hesitant, but Ayako leans into me. I caress her cheek. She pulls me closer. I study her porcelain face. It reminds me of an exquisite Noh mask. I touch her eyelashes and she blinks. I want to kiss her but dare not ruin everything. We gaze at each other for what seems like hours and she gently pulls me toward her. I feel the warmth of her breath against my cheek. I blush. She chuckles and kisses me lightly on my right cheek. I pull back. I've never been in love so this feels strange, like my body is floating in space. My head is spinning; my heart is pounding. I kiss her cheek, but she turns her head slightly so I accidentally kiss her lips. A shock wave shoots through my body. I stop, frozen like a statue. She laughs.

"This is your first time, isn't it?"

I nod. She pulls me toward her. I burrow into her hair, which flows over me in waves. I am totally at peace, like finding home. I never expected this when I offered to print her tattoo leg. It's funny how life works. You do things for people and suddenly you fall in love. My parents never told me about the ways of romance. They're so traditional and reserved around me. I'm a Maker at heart so I never expected anything like love.

Our cat-and-mouse battle with hackers continues week after week, like our secret romance. Steve launches a new cyber-security strategy, but the hackers find backdoors and deface everything. He patches the holes and comes up with a stronger defense, but the hackers find more new holes. It's a never-ending battle for supremacy, like video games.

Meanwhile, Ayako and I hustle to keep up with orders for her tattoo legs. She models her new designs, organizes tattoo fashion shows and photo shoots, takes orders and ships a new batch of designs. Steve battles to keep Tattoo City open for business but it's not easy. Our website has as many holes as Ayako's tattoo legs.

32

TATTOOVILLE

Tattoo wonderland
Surrounded by homeless folks
Give them a leg up!

Our Tattoo City is a total surprise. We have so many customers from around the world ordering our tattoo legs. I didn't know there were so many legless people. Brad and I look at the numbers and see many live in the Mideast, Africa, Asia, and Central America where are many wars. I never studied wars so it's new to me. Sometimes I stay up at night studying articles about war victims who have lost their legs and it pains me. I felt bad when I lost my leg, but at least I have wonderful parents, a home, food and friends. Many of these people have nothing. They live on the street like the homeless around town. What can I do to help? We're only a tiny company. We can't do much.

"Start small," says Steve. "I did when I launched Virtual Fillmore. I gave part-time marketing jobs for veterans having a tough time. They had a long learning curve since they didn't know anything about sales, but most do fine. You just have to trust and train them."

"How? Where?"

"Work with veteran and refugee groups. They know lots of members who have lost limbs. I see them all the time."

"Can you help us?"

"No problem. My Army buddies can introduce us. We just need to announce that Tattoo City is looking for veterans. The word will spread fast since there are so many vets who need jobs and better prosthetics."

"What do we need to do?"

"Just be yourself. Everyone knows your face. Just keep smiling. Let's create a video to invite vets to Tattoo City. But we shouldn't call it that. It sounds too big and impersonal."

"What do we call it?"

"Something smaller and friendly -- like Tattooville. Yeah, Tattooville sounds like a small village with friends, like SF. We need to make them feel at home."

"OK, Tattooville. Let's see what happens."

Within days, Steve's team creates a Tattooville with photos of veterans wearing their current prosthetic legs. They're big, ugly designs. No wonder they hide them under long pants. I would hide them too. Steve announces a kickoff meeting and many veterans show up – young, old, women, men and even late teens. I have never seen so my legless people in my life. Vets come up, hug me and thank me for the invitation. I am so happy. I'm no longer alone, but have many new friends who understand how I feel. We are a community. Steve was right. Tattooville is a better name than Tattoo City, which sounds too commercial. Our little tattoo village is for friends and their families.

My father is delighted by Tattooville and offers free space for veterans who want to learn 3D printing from Brad. Soon, our little workspace is filled with vets who print all sorts of legs, arms, hands and feet. They print cool designs of eagles, foxes, lions, bears, robots, singers and action characters. They remind me of J-Pop characters, but are based on Asian, African, and Latin American stories and myths. There are so many tattoo designs that we look like the "UN of Tattoos," which Mayor Tiffany proudly calls us.

Mayor Tiffany invites Navy veterans who lost their limbs in the Mideast. With Steve's Army buddies and her Navy friends, we look like an inter-service tattoo club, the first in the world. My father is so proud and invites Korean veterans to bridge the political gap between South Korea and Japan.

"Tattooville should be for everyone, not just Americans and Japanese, but for all nationalities," he says.

Mayor Tiffany and Steve agree, raising glasses of wine to celebrate our tiny achievement. We are small, but we make a big difference in the veterans' lives. I almost cry when I see their smiles and tears, remembering how I felt when Brad printed my first tattoo leg. It's strange how tattoo legs can bring people together. I never thought about tattoos, prosthetics, veterans and their families, just myself. Now I am becoming part of San Francisco. This is my new home and these veterans are my new family. We hug each other so much that I feel like a teddy bear. It's much more fun than always being unhappy and alone like in the past. At least we have fun creating and celebrating beautiful tattoo designs and parties.

I never want to leave my tattoo friends in San Francisco. I want to stay here forever! Tattoos rock!

33

QUANTUM COPS

In a land of crooks
The fast and stealthy survive
Quantum cyber sleuths!

I'm glad Steve and Ayako got Tattooville off the ground, but we still keep worrying about cyber-security since our site is constantly being attacked by scammers, phishers and ransomware crooks. I didn't know protecting websites was so difficult. Mayor Tiffany helps by involving intelligence agencies to watch our back, but it's still a cops-and-robbers challenge. No matter what defenses we create, the hackers find ways to circumvent them and penetrate our website. We're so exhausted since it keeps us up at night.

"Don't worry," says Mayor Tiffany. "We're bringing in the howitzers."

"Howitzers?" I ask. "What's that?"

"Quantum cyber-security with the latest AI tools."

"It's sounds like cyber war. We're just a tiny website."

"All commerce is cyber war today. Either we plug the holes or hackers will permanently shut us down. I don't want all of our initiatives to crash and burn. That's a no-no in the Navy. Everyone is watching the City so we cannot fail."

"Yes, admiral!"

Within days, Mayor Tiffany brings in the howitzers – the top cyber-war experts from the Pentagon, her old buddies, who know every trick in the books. They plug every hole and backdoor so effectively that we are totally amazed.

"How in the world did they do it so fast?" asks Steve, who

shakes his head with disbelief. "My Virtual Fillmore is always being attacked by hackers. I can't figure out how to stop them."

"My team will help you. The City needs every penny of sales and taxes so we need help all small businesses in town. In fact, I'm setting cyber-security workshops and technical assistance for all City businesses."

That's what I love about Mayor Tiffany and her Pentagon bros. They are can-do folks who know how to stop cyber crooks. I want to be like them. We Makers can make nearly anything, except advanced quantum computers, so we are totally vulnerable to cyber attacks. Our sites always go down like ducks in a shooting gallery.

I want to ask Mayor Tiffany if she would recommend me for the Naval Academy so I can learn cool stuff like her. At least it would be free so my poor mom would not have to worry about my tuition. My younger sister Yumi at Cal is draining our little savings so I need to work and find scholarships. Since dad died, our Kimono Minds shop has struggled to stay afloat so any scholarships and loans would help. Maybe I can join the Navy's quantum cyber-security teams and work with Japan's self-defense forces. That would be super cool. Then I could polish my Japanese and build useful stuff to keep the peace. I could work with one of the biggest teams of cyber cops in the world.

I ask Steve if he would mention my interest in the Navy. Within days, Mayor Tiffany emails me a glowing recommendation and the admissions committee replies that they like my rare achievements. They need more robotics experts. I hope it helps me get into West Point!

I'm so excited that I tell my mom who tells her Kyoto friends. Even though I'm not accepted to West Point yet, they invite me to visit them. Mom hints they will introduce me to charming young ladies. I don't have the heart to mention Ayako, but that doesn't matter. I may go to West Point! I'm crossing my fingers. If I get in, mom can breathe easier. I would get a great education and duty in Japan. How great would that be!

What do I tell Ayako? She's helping me with Robotville so leaving for West Point would ruin everything. Should I go or stay? What if she joins me at a nearby college? Would her parents agree?

34

TATTOOS ALL THE WAY

Life goes its own way
Like seagulls taking to flight
Street cats brawl at night

Life is so cruel. First, I lost my leg, now Brad wants to study at West Point. Why now? Why so far away? He might as well be half way around the world. Now I will be left alone to run Tattooville without his help. Can I do it? Why can't he stay? He could enroll at Cal with his sister Yumi. Maybe he can get a scholarship, anything but West Point. That would be silent torture for me. He's like my left arm; without him, I feel lost. I'm shy around guys but he's different. I love his smile and willingness to help others. I'm no Disney princess but I do believe in magic. He has a way of magically bringing objects and people to life. Why does he want to leave? How can I urge him to stay so we can build Tattooville?

My father agrees with me, but my mother says to let him go. I'm too young; it's just puppy love. I can meet other guys. I know lots of nice guys, but they're not the same. They like making stuff but not helping others as much. They lack Brad's magic and charm. That's why I cannot let him go. The City needs him; my father needs him; I need him. How can I persuade him to stay?

I talk with my father who wants to help but he's busy trying to keep our bank afloat.

"Couldn't you set up a scholarship fund for him and others?" I ask. "Even a little bit would help him stay here."

"I know you like him, but it's difficult."

"You mean, impossible. You won't even try."

"I didn't say that. I want to help him."

"Then set up a foundation."

"We don't have the money. Where will it come from?"

"Tattooville. You and Brad will help me generate more sales with the help of your friends."

"How?"

"By sponsoring a Tattoo Expo with your friends."

"Expo? Do you know how much that will cost?"

"Do you want Brad to stay or not? Or do you want me to leave if he goes east?"

"Are you silly? You need your mother and me."

"We can open Tattooville near West Point. There are lots of veterans on the East Coast who could use our prosthetic tattoo legs."

"You're not serious."

"More than ever. Will you support us?"

My father looks at me with disbelief. I have never demanded anything from him, but this is serious. Without Brad, Tattooville is dead. Akihabara West is dead. He brings both to life; he brings me to life. He created my leg and those for others. He absolutely cannot leave. I will not let him leave. He can study here and rebuild downtown into the Tattoo Capital with me. We are a team, like my father and me. Without us, Little Osaka, Akihabara and Tattooville are all dead. As he always reminds me, it's the puppeteers who bring life to puppets.

My mother disagrees but she finally concedes. We will help Brad stay in SF. We will help his mother with her Kimono Minds shop and Brad with his Makerville, which will be in the lower floors of Kabuki Bank. We will all be one happy family together with our SF friends.

When Brad hears from my father, he rushes to see me.

"I can't afford it," says Brad. "I may get a full scholarship to West Point."

"We'll help you study at Cal with your sister. It's closer and we need you."

"What about my future? I could serve in Japan."

"You can study cyber security at Cal and work with Mayor Tiffany's Pentagon buddies here. It's easier. You'll be closer to the action at home."

"But I want to travel."

"You can do it through business. I'll help you."

"You don't know anything about international business."

"My father can teach us. We can build Tattoville into a global brand, starting in Japan and Asia."

"What do you mean 'we'? I thought you had to stay with your parents."

"Steve says our Tattooville website is getting lots of hits from Asia."

"So you're thinking..."

"Robotville and Tattooville are intertwined."

Brad's face turns pale. I love it when he looks surprised. He's like a little kid getting a birthday present.

"But what West Point? What about touring Asia?"

"Forget West Point. You have me."

"You? Are you crazy? Have you told your parents?"

"My dad agrees. We all need you. Steve's veteran friends think we have the coolest mission. Better than shooting others."

Brad gulps. He's so cute when he does that. He reminds me of my girlfriend in Osaka. He's like a kid. I'm six months older so I can be his big sister!

Brad needs convincing but finally wakes up and realizes the City needs him more than the Navy. They can always find sailors but they can't find Makers who can create things and magically bring people to life. He's the ultimate puppeteer like his father and his Bunraku friends. We should invite them. They would liven up the City and wake up Makers who only think about robots. The best robots are Bunraku puppets. They are like real people. In the hands of experts, they become alive. Together, we will revive downtown with our Bunraku puppets, robots, avatars and dolls.

35

BUNRAKU BOTS

Lifeless as robots
Souls lying disembodied
Jumping up alive!

Ayako has a way to selling you anything. First, she asks me to 3D print her a prosthetic leg and asks for a fancy tattoo design. Then she asks me to help her create a prosthetics demo and pop-up shop. Next, Tattooville. Now an entire universe of tattoo legs and puppets. I'm just a Maker but she wants me to be a magician. I can't work miracles; I just build stuff.

"You're such a wimp," she says. "Just lifeless robots that you need to program like a PC. That's not interesting. You need to bring them to life."

"How, smarty?"

"Like a Bunraku puppeteer, like your father."

I blanche since it's been months since I last thought about my father who made Bunraku puppets when I was a kid. It was his passion that he acquired when he studied in Osaka where he met my mom at a kimono fashion show using Bunraku. They were an odd couple: a crazy Kyoto kimono designer and an aspiring Bunraku puppet maker from San Francisco. Inspired by an Osaka University professor of Bunraku, they would create short Bunraku plays with puppets dressed in gorgeous kimonos designed by my mother. They were a hit in town. People came from all over to see their Bunraku kimono fashion shows with puppets of all shapes and sizes – kids, elders, sexy ladies and sumo wrestlers. Mom was smart; she sold a lot of kimonos, not just miniature Bunraku dolls. We still have photos and videos of their over-the-top performances. My dad imagined himself a Japanese Jim Henson. My mom wanted to be the Yohji Yamamoto of cool kimonos. They were cool. Our house was always a total, upside-down mess with kimonos and puppets piled all over the place so it was hard to walk around without tripping. But after my father died, the craziness ended. Kimono Minds became a quiet kimono shop without the zaniness of my dad. My sisters – Mari, Emi and Yumi – and I miss him a lot, but mom soldiers on. We became the coolest kimono shop in the Bay Area, but now it's lifeless like my dad's puppets lying around mom's workshop.

Ayako wants to bring his puppets back to life. She wants Little Osaka to bring downtown back to life; she wants to bring my family back to life. For her, it's about returning favors since I helped her and her dad. Mom calls it "ongaeshi" – the heavy obligation to return favors. She wants to do it with Bunraku puppets, prosthetics and kimonos. Talk about a weird combination, just like my family. But all's fair in life and business so we might as well go for it. SF's downtown is dead as my dad's puppets so we might as well bring it back to life by becoming its new puppeteers. Politicians and realtors aren't doing it fast enough. Imagine that; using puppets and robots to revive downtown. We have no choice. We either put on awesome performances or our Kabuki Bank, Little Osaka, and Tattooville will end in quiet deaths, something Mayor Tiffany, Steve, my father, Ayako and I will never let happen as long as we're in charge. We will do anything to bring the City back to life. I will do anything to help Ayako and her father. I will do anything to bring my father's spirit back to his puppets, even if it means not going to West Point.

Ayako, her Tattooville friends and my Maker buddies huddle over strategy. What are we going to do? What's the fastest, cheapest and easiest way to grab media attention and visitors to downtown? We need something spectacular.

A Bunraku Bot Festival! You're probably wondering: What's that? It's a seamless merging of my father's Bunraku puppets with my robots and Ayako's Tattooville prosthetics. What does that look like? Ayako and I meet with my sisters Mari and Emi to get their opinions.

"You definitely need Goth tattoos," says Mari, sporting her latest leather jumpsuit. "I'll get my biker designers to create the coolest designs for your Biker Bots."

"Biker Bots?"

"Yeah, hot Bunraku bikers wearing cool Goth jackets with wild Japanese tattoo designs on their backs and legs. That should grab everyone's attention."

"How long will it take?"

"A week. I'll get my best friend to print big tattoos for my line of recycled leather jackets of all colors."

"Like Pride Week?"

"Exactly, a bigger market and we'll get all genders behind us. We can't be biased. People expect cool, surprising and inclusive stuff, not the same old biker designs. I think Bunraku puppets on big and small bikes would look cool."

"How big?"

"Like eight feet tall. You said you can 3D print anything."

"But why that big?"

"Bigger margins."

"So giant Bunraku biker bots?"

"And autonomous bikes."

"A-bikes? How?"

"That's in your court, genius. I'll bring the designers and bikers. You bring the AI and autonomous vehicle experts."

How am I supposed to work magic doing something I've never done before? None of my buddies have ever done anything remotely similar before. We'll have to make it up on the fly.

"What do you think, Emi?" I ask. "Does that sound possible? You've got the biggest designer group."

"Totally doable," she replies. "We've already done it without much money and mostly volunteers -- Akiharabara West, Little Osaka, Goth City, Maker Village, Soul City, Cosplay City, J-Pop and K-Pop City, or Tattooville. Anything is possible. I'll post online. We'll probably get hundreds of cosplay designers. They just need clear instructions. What do you guys want to do first?"

Ayako and I sit back, mulling over idea, then she jumps up and goes to the whiteboard.

"I want the coolest Bunraku biker dolls first. Brad, you print the dolls. Mari, you provide the small leather jackets and jumpsuits. Ayako and I will provide the Goth tattoo designs."

"What about the big bikers?"

"After we sell the small ones. We need to save some

surprises for our fans. It will be a crescendo of biker designs."

Our mouths drop open. Emi sounds crazier than my mom and Ayako.

Our little workshop in Tattooville comes to life. First, my Maker bros and I move our 3D printers from our Robotville so we can all work together. Next, I bring some of my father's Bunraku puppets so we can scan them in. Next, Mari downloads motorcycle designs from her digital library. We pick a few hot machines and print out small versions about six inches high. Soon, Tattooville is filled with dozens of cool machines of all sizes.

Next, I print out various types of Bunraku bots – young women and guys, old guys, and teens. Mari provides the jackets and jumpsuits. Emi's cosplay design friends add scarves and fluffy collars. We line them up along the window in Kabuki Bank's gallery so visitors can see them, then we post photos online.

Overnight, we are packed with sightseers and buyers. Visitors pile out of BART like fans going to the SF Giants and Warriors games. Everyone is stunned. The kids run into our shop and beg their parents to buy them our bots. We price them under a hundred dollars to make them affordable and they sell out in hours, so we print more to avoid disappointing people.

"This is nuts," says Mari. "I never thought people would buy Bunraku biker dolls, just Barbie."

"Barbie is so last century. Wait until we print out the big Bunraku biker bots and dolls. You'll see who the real fanatics are."

Seeing the sales rush, my Maker bros print out hundreds of small bots and dozens of big bots. They sell out in hours so we ramp up production. This Bunraku Bot rage probably won't last long so we need to strike while sales are hot.

But the sales don't dry up. Mayor Tiffany is so jazzed by our mini-revival that she dresses up in a recycled biker jumpsuit from her "Top Gun" Navy fighter pilot days, which goes totally viral. We are swamped in orders for fighter pilot jackets with cool tattoo designs of lions and tigers and California bears, oh my!

"Hit 'em when they least expect it," she laughs, modeling for journalists.

The media loves Mayor Tiffany. She has no qualms about selling San Francisco. She leverages the hell out of her Top Gun fame to regenerative fashion, biker tattoos and prosthetics.

"As a child, my dream was to model in LA."

"You can do it here and in LA if you lose the election."

"No way! The City is more fun. We can try weird stuff that LA folks laugh at. And SF lovers expect creativity out of the City, not just tech commuters. We need our artists and crazies to revive it – like your dad's Bunraku puppets."

"Burning Man!" shouts Mari. "That will set the streets on fire!"

"The fire department would never allow it so let's use LEDs.

"Then LED light shows along Market Street and the Embarcadero! That would bring out huge audiences. Let's invite Yoko Hamabe. Her dancing solar sculptures would grab worldwide coverage."

"I've always wanted to attend Burning Man," says Ayako. "But my parents never let me go to the desert. Too wild."

"We'll bring the desert to the City. After all, they began at Baker Beach until the City kicked them out."

"Talk about irony," I say. "SF kicks out Burning Man which ultimately saves it from bankruptcy."

"Anything goes," says Mari. "We've got to move fast before this Buraku Bot craze ends."

"All systems are go," says Ayako. "Houston, this is San Francisco. The recovery has launched."

Ayako salutes a photo of Mayor Tiffany and the American and Japanese flags flying in bank's gallery. We all laugh. This is going to be fun. Imagine that, Burning Man artists and fans lighting up downtown. This will be one of the greatest shows on Earth.

36

BURNING CITY

Designers descend
upon an empty City
Burners come alive!

The greatest show on Earth is an understatement. I knew San
Francisco were crazy and weird, but not this weird. Within weeks,
Mari involves her Burning Man buddies who Mayor Tiffany invites to
design the Independence Day street designs. They are not like typical
designers, but do amazing stuff. This is why I came to San Francisco.
They do stuff that no Japanese would ever consider in downtown.
Even our Gion Festival looks old and dated by comparison.

My parents and I watch as Mari's Burning Man friends create
huge LED sculptures of all sorts – Japanese temples and huge
Godzillas in honor of Kabuki Bank and Ayatusch Ohlone families,
Californio ranch owners, Mission fathers, stagecoaches, gold miners,
Chinese railroad builders, Fillmore jazz musicians, women in
Victorian dresses, 1930 labor strikers, 1960s Summer of Love hippies
in gowns and bellbottom jeans, Filipino stick dancers, Korean
maidens, mariachi singers, Carnaval dancers, rainbow Pride outfits,
and Tenderloin seniors in recycled suits – the entire history of San
Francisco in one long line going from city hall down Market Street
past Kabuki Bank to the Ferry Building and along the Embarcadero
to UCSF Mission Bay in the south to Fishermen's Wharf in the
north. The gigantic LED sculptures are so amazing that BART is
overloaded with passengers around the clock both weekend and
weekdays. Our sales go through the roof. Every City artist and
busker is in the streets selling out. Business is booming. Small
merchants are cheering. The City looks like one non-stop shopping

mall and outdoor festival, with music and dance and regenerative fashion shows led by Mayor Tiffany. Our visitors are stunned by the beauty. We are all cheering.

The Japanese media interviews my mother who is in tears, crying for the first time in my life. She bows deeply to Mayor Tiffany who awards the City's honorary citizen awards to my father and mother, Brad, Mari, Emi, Yumi, me and our friends. I am crying since Brad prints out big golden heart necklaces and places them around the necks of my father, mother and me. I look at him through my tears, unable to stop crying. I want to hug him forever. I never want to let go of him or the City. I want to stay here forever. I want to leave my heart here.

37

SITTING ON THE DOCK

Seagulls soar above
Far above maddening crowds
Like Buddhas we sit

So that's how we saved downtown. Who would have ever thought a Japanese bank going bankrupt would have been the catalyst? Who would have guessed a girl who lost her leg would have been the inspiration for all of us? As my buddies remind me: "The football usually bounces the wrong way." But often the wrong way is the only way to wake you up, instead of just sitting around moping and complaining. Sometimes the prospect of utter defeat is the only way to make you hustle. Given life's messiness, you can remain lifeless like my father's Bunraku puppets lying around the house or become the puppeteer of your life.

It's hard without my dad. When I'm down, I often play with his puppets for hours, remembering his crazy antics and laughter filling the house. I pretend that I am a crazy puppeteer like him reincarnated as a crazy robot Maker. I am the robot; I am the puppet; I am the puppeteer; I am him. Then I plunge into my ideal world of spine-tingling robots and dolls, like his world of beautiful, spunky Bunraku puppets that picked me up when I was down and ready to give up and play like a kid again. We are our parents' spirit, no matter where we go in life. We carry them with us everywhere.

Meanwhile, I have a lot to look forward to. Ayako is my goddess and inspiration. It's sad she lost her leg, but without her accident, we never would have met and I never would have printed her tattoo leg. We never would have built Little Osaka, Tattooville and my little Robot City. Kawahara-san would never have kept

Kabuki Bank open and supported our pet projects. But he believes in all of us so it's been one hell of a rocket ride. Maybe the City can recover like my puppets and Ayako's tattoo buddies. Maybe we can reimagine the City as a bio-circular city like Asian cities are doing today. Perhaps I can study at Cal and realize my dream of becoming one of the top prosthetic exoskeleton designers.

So I've decided: forget West Point! I'll earn my way through Cal so I can be with Ayako to rebuild the City, one 3D-printed brick by brick. We will turn lifeless buildings into magical stages filled with love and laughter and commerce. We will create our virtual and real world fantasyland. We will create the future in our imaginations, with puppets, robots, prosthetics, music, food and fashions. Nothing will stop us, only our imaginations.

After work, Ayako and I often go to Pier 7, my favorite pier in the City, to hang out and enjoy a panoramic view of the downtown, Coit Tower, Treasure Island, the Bay Bridge all lit up, ferries coming in and out, and freighters pulling into the port of Oakland. We are blessed to live in this magnificent corner of the universe, listening to my favorite song, "Sitting on the Dock by the Bay." If I were a musician, I would play it everyday, but I'm just a Maker so I'll let my robots do the performing for me. They have spirit like my father's puppets so I'll let them dance and boogie and sing to their hearts' content. And we will sit on the dock, watching the sun vanish over North Beach and light up the Berkeley hills with golden flecks of light, and enjoy the fog rolling in. We will be the fog and light and water. We will find home again.

THE END

ABOUT THE AUTHOR

Sheridan Tatsuno is a San Francisco writer and principal of Dreamscape Global, a writer, media producer, publisher, urban planner, business adviser, and serial entrepreneur who specializes in virtual reality (VR) for urban design, commerce and storytelling. He is advising tech start-ups (Aimedis.io and Regenerate.is) and co-launching a new media studio to provide VR solutions for designing, showcasing and building healthy cities. www.dreamscapeglobal.com

Trained in urban planning at Harvard's Graduate School of Design, Sheridan has worked as an urban planner in housing, public transit and major energy projects before shifting to high-tech market research and consulting at Dataquest in 1983. He is a fiction writer who began with short stories, novels, and poetry, then applied his storytelling to two business books produced for television: "The Technopolis Strategy" (Prentice Hall, 1986) about Japan's 26 science cities, which was produced as "Japan Dreaming" by Central Independent Television plc (1991) and aired throughout the Commonwealth; and "Created in Japan" (HarperCollins, 1990) about creative Japanese product design, which was used for the Kyoto scenes in the 4-hour PBS series "The Creative Spirit" (1992). He has written 18 screenplays and 12 novels.

His "Virtually San Francisco" sci-fi comedy series features 10 novels (available on Amazon) exploring VR for designing homeless shelters, entertainment, shopping, STEAM (STEM + Arts) education, space/time travel, and medicine. These novels were inspired by his work with a Swedish startup that used VR to design Copenhagen Malmo Port, Lund 2070, Malmo and Stockholm (2016-2020) with the Unreal 4.0 Engine. Aimedis uses Unreal 5.0 for its Healthy Cities platform.

His professional Linkedin articles about VR for sustainable cities, retail, STEAM education and medicine are available at:
https://www.linkedin.com/in/statsuno/detail/recent-activity/posts/

For details, contact: smtatsuno@gmail.com

www.ingramcontent.com/pod-product-compliance
Lightning Source LLC
Chambersburg PA
CBHW062324290526
45794CB00005B/1882